# MONTESSORI TODDLER DISCIPLINE

A Guide for Parents to Raising Independent and Well-Educated Kids with No-Drama

## MAGGIE GARDNER

First published in the United States of America in 2020

ISBN 9798690700652

INTRODUCTION.................................................7

SENSITIVE PERIODS ........................................12

THE "ABSORBENT MIND"..............................36

BASIC PRINCIPLES ........................................40

MONTESSORI HOME......................................59

DAILY ROUTINES...........................................83

PARENTS AND EDUCATION........................ 113

EFFECTIVE COMMUNICATION .................. 138

ACTIVITIES FOR KIDS .................................176

A LETTER TO PARENTS............................... 199

REFERENCE ................................................. 201

# HOW TO READ AND USE THIS BOOK

This book has been created to guide parents in discovering the Montessori approach to raising independent, curious, and well-educated kids.

It will include some basic principles and many suggestions to apply them in everyday life.

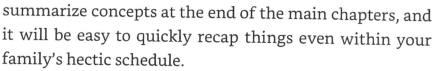

To facilitate learning, it will summarize concepts at the end of the main chapters, and it will be easy to quickly recap things even within your family's hectic schedule.

Some days you will be able to follow Montessori's teachings to the letter; sometimes, it will be an outstanding achievement to just making it to the end of the day. Please forgive yourself and allow enough time to absorb these new concepts and implement them in your routines.

# INTRODUCTION

"Within the child lies the fate of the future."

— Maria Montessori

**M**ontessori method refers to a philosophy of learning and education that was developed by Italian physician Maria Montessori.

Born in 1870 in Chiaravalle, Italy, Maria Montessori has exhibited a strong personality since childhood. At a young age, she intended to become an engineer and attended a technical school, even though her father disapproved, then studied medicine at the University of Rome.

In 1896 she graduated from the University of Rome La Sapienza Medical School, becoming the first female physician in Italy.

Montessori then joined the University of Rome's Psychiatric Clinic, where she increased her psychiatry, education, and anthropology knowledge.

She devoted her first years to children with special needs and mental challenges, for whom she specifically developed specific education theories. Becoming the director of the Scuola Ortofrenica, an institution dedicated to mentally disabled children, she had the opportunity to test her ideas and prove a remarkable improvement of the children under her care in reading and writing, even surpassing average achievement scores.

In 1907, Montessori opened the now-famous Casa Dei Bambini, or Children's House, a revolutionary school experiment in Rome's low-income housing project. Starting from the basic principle of her philosophy, the "spontaneous self-development" of children, Montessori created an environment to allow children to learn and develop their skills at their own pace.

The teacher's role became discovering each child's potential, and following their lead in the process of learning, changing dramatically from what was considered standard for that time.

The children's ability to absorb knowledge and concentrate on learning soon became widely accepted worldwide, and the Casa de Bambini became the basis for what is now known as the Montessori method.

Montessori's natural learning method's impressive results soon brought fame and invitations to travel worldwide. In 1913, she visited the United States for the first time, where she had strong supporters, like Thomas Edison and Alexander Graham Bell.

In 1915, Montessori was invited to set up a glass-walled classroom the Panama-Pacific Exposition in San Francisco, where spectators could observe twenty-one children, all new to the Montessori method, developing their innate potential through specific activities. The exhibition was so successful that it won two gold medals for education and focused the world's attention on Montessori's innovative method.

Maria Montessori traveled worldwide for over 40 years, establishing training courses, lecturing, writing, and promoting her learning method.

Nominated for the Nobel Peace Prize three times, she moved to the Netherlands in 1949, where she lived until her passing in 1952.

Her lifetime work of observation of children and their abilities to grow and learn is still very appreciated internationally. Many organizations promote her method, and Montessori schools are spread in both the United States and worldwide.

Whether you are evaluating a Montessori school for your child or not, this guide will explain Montessori's fundamental principles and will help you implement them in your everyday life.

In this way, the family, a focal point in children's development, will be promoting their freedom to become more focused and creative as they grow intellectually and emotionally.

# MARIA MONTESSORI — QUICK RECAP

♡ **First female** physician in Italy in 1896.

♡ Applied her theories of education on **children with special needs**.

♡ **Different style of teaching**, never seen before.

♡ Goal: discover the **potential of each child** and follow their lead in the process of learning.

♡ Nominated for the **Nobel Peace Prize** three times, passed away in 1952.

♡ Her lifetime work of **observation of children** and their abilities to grow and learn is still very appreciated **internationally**.

# CHAPTER 1

# SENSITIVE PERIODS

"There is no man existing who has not been formed by
the child he once was."

— Maria Montessori

Every child is born with billions of brain cells, and
from birth, a large number of connections between
those brain cells are made, thanks to the child's
unconscious experiences. This process is very active until
six years of age, so the most important thing parents can
do is to provide an environment set up to nurture this
process. By doing this, we directly influence our

children's brain development and their ability to learn. Introducing children to learning opportunities every day will help them become happy, well-adjusted adults.

This intense development cycle is made of different stages, and the completion of each one has different timings for every kid. Maria Montessori compares children to sprouting seeds: everyone differs from the others and grows at its own rate.

Kid's development stages, or "sensitive periods" as Montessori calls them, are phases where the child instinctively moves towards a well-defined kind of experience, which allows him to grow intellectually and physically.

They are essential and necessary to help kids acquire specific abilities and traits crucial for their development and well-being. Sensitive periods are all tied together, and each one acts as a base for the next.

Recognizing and supporting sensitive periods in your kid's development begins with a knowledge of what is typical at different ages. The other aspect is merely observing your kids and allowing them to progress at their own pace.

To support your children during this particular time of learning, it is essential to provide them with a supportive learning environment that offers stimuli appropriate to their development stage.

Since this book is not intended for parents already mastering an in-depth knowledge of pedagogy and the Montessori method in particular, we will look at the main sensitive periods simplifying the basic concepts of Maria Montessori's philosophy.

The main sensitive periods are:

♡ Movement and coordination

♡ Sensory awareness and exploration

♡ Language

♡ Sense of order

♡ Social skills and good manners

♡ Music

♡ Writing

♡ Reading

♡ Mathematics

# MOVEMENT AND COORDINATION

From birth to 4 years of age, children live a sensitive period involving movement, which includes exploring the space they are allowed to (usually starting from the house) and manipulating materials within it. Movement enables children to explore a setting with ease, keeping them excited and eager to physically explore their way around.

Preparing and encouraging your kid during this period will ensure steady development in hand-eye coordination and fine motor skills, essential for writing, and many other crucial abilities.

An active child is essentially developing their gross motor skills required to move the larger muscles in the arms, legs, and body, for example, to walk, run, throw, lift, and kick. With movement, a child develops body awareness, a sense of coordination, reaction, speed, balance, and strength.

## SENSORY AWARENESS AND EXPLORATION

Children refine their senses between birth and five years of age. This sensitive period shows a kid's fascination with sensory experiences, touch in particular, but also taste, sight, and smell.

The first sensory awareness phase occurs from one to three years of age and is related to small objects. This period is characterized by a keen interest in small items and tiny details.

The second phase, sensory exploration, occurs from 2.5 to 6 years. This phase can be defined by an intense desire to take part in learning experiences that integrate the senses. Children learn a system to classify objects within their environment thanks to these experiences and improve their fine and gross motor skills.

To support this sensitive period, it is crucial to provide your kid with many opportunities to explore their environment through their senses. At home, you could provide your kid with opportunities to group objects with similar traits and describe materials with different textures. Have a look at Chapter 8 for more ideas.

# LANGUAGE

Language development starts at seven months into pregnancy and continues until the child is six years old. However, the learning period for spoken language is fundamentally between seven months in the womb to 2

½ years of age. By that time, the kid is usually communicating in short sentences.

You can do several things to get the most out of your kid's sensitive period for spoken language. For example, everyday activities and experiences are an occasion to engage in a conversation with the child.

Using a vast vocabulary from the start is very useful to the kid to absorb a variety of words. At the beginning, it will be an unconscious process. From 3 years old on, it will become conscious. More on this in the next Chapter on "Absorbent Mind."

Reading together is also a significant activity. Choosing books with big pictures and few words usually create a strong interest in the kid. We have the occasion to consolidate a good habit and also expand our child's vocabulary. The best thing to do, as always, is to let the child choose the subject. Keep in mind that books illustrating everyday life situations are usually preferred during the first years as the child cannot separate real life from fantasy. The child may find scary some themes that may seem to us very attractive (e.g., monsters).

This is a stage of progressive learning, and it's essential to allow your kid ample time and opportunities to interact with you. Bear in mind that the child may need some time to learn to express their needs.

Just be patient and try not to anticipate them. It may be tempting to do what's easier in that moment, but it's certainly not the best. Think long term.

Wait for your kid to gesture or speak before getting what they want. After your kid attempts to communicate, help him modeling correct speech if needed.

For example, if your kid is complaining because they are thirsty, the easy way to eliminate the crying is to give them the glass. However, the best way is to withhold a bit and say, "Do you want a drink?" or "say, 'water.'" Once the kid attempts to communicate, tell, "Great asking! I'm going to get you some water."

♡ **SENSITIVE PERIODS** 21

This way, slower than merely fulfilling your child's need with no effort for them, encourages your kid. They did their best to express their needs and got the result. Give your kid your full attention when they are talking to you.

Watch your facial expressions and body language, and be sure to look interested by showing enthusiasm. Soon your kid will communicate correctly thanks to your support.

# SENSE OF ORDER

Children have an innate sense of order, and this can be noticed in many things. For example, a well-studied routine for activities that repeat identical almost every day (like morning routine: waking up, having breakfast, brushing teeth, getting dressed, and go to school) is usually beneficial and helps the kid understand what happens and know what they have to do next. This knowledge enhances their sense of security, which is particularly crucial during this sensitive period.

**MONTESSORI TODDLER DISCIPLINE** ♡

In the Montessori method, every item has its place in the house, helping develop the child's independence. If everything the child needs, like clothes, shoes, materials, and so on, are easily accessible and easy to put back on their place, they will be stimulated to do things without help.

Until this period is not completed, you will notice that changes are not welcome and could cause some discomfort in the child. This is perfectly normal, and our role is to support them while they learn to cope.

# SOCIAL SKILLS AND GOOD MANNERS

A child learns to be part of a group between 2 and 5 years old. During this period, they develop a strong interest in social relationships and learn to interact correctly with others.

This is the stage of growth where children learn to develop friendships and participate in cooperative play. The sensitive period is an appropriate stage to introduce the importance of manners and basic human interaction principles.

To support social skills development in your kids, it is essential to provide them with opportunities to socialize with other children. It's vital that we, as parents, model positive social behaviors and practice grace and courtesy rituals such as saying "please" and "thank you."

Kids are watching, and they usually model what they are exposed to. So our role is definitely one of the most significant inputs they will process when creating their approach to others.

Maria Montessori believed that for the world to become a more peaceful and more civilized society, the new generations must learn to live in harmony, and their hidden potential must be developed to the fullest. That's why her method is centered on preparing the kid for life in society, teaching to collaborate with others, and promoting essential skills such as responsibility, concentration, and perseverance.

She also believed that a kid needs to learn to be caring and compassionate towards others.

## OLDER SISTERS AND BROTHERS INTERACTION

Family is a miniature world where healthy interactions take place. Children do not need constant verbal reminders about behavior from adults, and this happens mainly for two reasons. We already talked about children taking us as an example, but let's not forget the vital role of older sisters or brothers who live those rules as well. Younger children learn by example from them too.

Also, older children are usually keen to offer help to the younger siblings, and by giving that help, they become better and stronger individuals. The sense of responsibility they take over is impressive and a huge asset in their personal development.

Receiving help comes naturally to younger children. In turn, they offer support to older siblings, too, learning essential skills for their growth.

# MUSIC

Children are naturally interested in music, and there are many reasons why it is so attractive. For example, music is a language, and children are oriented toward language learning.

It also evokes movement, and children enjoy it and need it for their growth.

Music stimulates neural pathways associated with higher intelligence forms as abstract thinking, empathy, and mathematics by engaging the brain. It's also a creative experience that allows children to release their emotions. They need it dramatically, especially when still learning to express themselves.

Its rhythmic patterns help develop memory and train children's listening skills. Good listening skills and school achievements go hand in hand.

Music is a social activity that involves family and community participation. Children love to sing and dance at home, school, and at church. This increases their personal and social awareness leading them to be more easily socialized.

Montessori indicated that exposure to music (listening, learning, and playing) has beneficial effects for preschoolers. She promoted active musical training to improve their problem-solving skills, physical coordination, self-confidence, concentration, memory, visual, and language skills.

For a maximum benefit, the musical training experience should begin before the age of 5. The window of opportunity, to increase and strengthen neural bridges, stays open until about ten years old.

# WRITING

Kids start their approach to writing by scribbling and doodling, fascinated by just being able to make a mark on a piece of paper.

Pencil grip is prepared from a very young age through toys that engage the thumb and the first two fingers: from tiny knobbed puzzle pieces to building sets; there are endless ways to keep things fun and stimulating for every kid.

A child around 4 and 4 ½ years is usually ready to learn the alphabet letters, starting from their phonetic sounds.

The Montessori method uses a straightforward yet very effective way to teach the alphabet: sandpaper letters.

Sandpaper letters are written in lower case script and mounted on wooden support of two colors: blue for consonants and pink for vowels.

The child learns to write in 3 steps.

In the first step, the parent (or teacher) shows three letters to the child, one by one, and repeats its phonetic equivalent several times while tracing the letter itself with index and middle finger.

The kid learns the letter's sound and, at the same time, learns how to trace it without using a pen, associating both things thanks to the tactile stimulus of the sandpaper. This sets the muscle coordination, so when the kid starts practicing writing with a pen, they will already know how to trace the letters.

In the second step, the parent (or teacher) will ask the kid to pick one letter by pronouncing the phonetic equivalent (e.g., for "S": "Pick "ssss" and trace it"). In this way, the kids will further consolidate the association between phonics and written signs.

In the third step, the parent (or teacher) chooses a letter from the three available and asks the child to trace it and tell what letter is.

As always, observation of the child is essential to understand when they are ready to add another group of 3 letters, then other 3, etc.

Of course, these are just the first steps to introducing the sandpaper letters. It will take some time and patience to let children learn all the alphabet, but it will be worth it.

# READING

A child usually starts to read between the ages of 4 ½ to 5 ½ years old. Reading is a challenging, multi-step task that must be effectively instructed and learned. Recent technological discoveries confirmed what Maria Montessori had already clear: how the brain learns to read.

New readers use one area of the brain to connect the phonetic sounds and the related letters and then combine them into words. It's a process that requires some time to set up, which is why kids figuring out how to read learn to do it gradually. Then, after a period that varies from child to child, a new brain area starts to dominate.

This area allows the kid to build a permanent archive of the most frequent, familiar words that can be perceived immediately. This empowers them to read by observing the entire word directly, without separating sounds one by one. Kids with dyslexia or other learning incapacities can't make a smooth change between single sounds and complete words and should be supported accordingly.

Maria Montessori perceived that spoken language and written language are clearly related. While verbal language acquisition happens subconsciously (that is, the child is too young to be aware of it), written language acquisition and reading are a conscious process.

Montessori also observed that after acquiring the essential phonetic sounds, reading becomes natural. From the very foundation of writing, a kid develops the ability to read and seldom the other way around.

We use around 5,000 words consistently, and another 10,000 less regularly, for a total of 15,000 "common words." A way to improve this number is reading as much as possible. The more you read, the greater your vocabulary.

It's simpler for children to pronounce a word they have already heard than a new word. This is why it's essential to spend some time every day to read to your kid from a very young age. It's also important to stimulate their reading capacities by allowing them to read alone when ready.

Begin with simple books, including single words that boost your kid's confidence before moving on to phrases. Phonetic reading sets are also excellent reinforcements for early readers.

Reading games that use the alphabet's phonetic sounds to blend and form 3-4 letter words are beneficial to train persistence and patience in the child while completing the learning process of reading.

# MATHEMATICS

Numbers and math are present in many everyday activities from a young age. Learning to tell the time? That's math. Playing hide and seek and counting backward? That's math. Sharing your snack with a friend? Math, again.

Montessori had a visionary yet convenient idea of teaching math, where kids move from a physical perception of numbers and concepts to an abstract vision and reasoning.

To do that, kids use several materials appropriate for their age, the most famous being the golden beads.

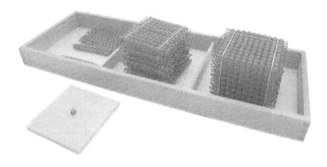

The aim of the golden beads is to teach the decimal system: units, tens, hundreds, and thousands. One golden bead is a unit. They can be single, arranged in rows of 10, squares of 100, and cubes of 1.000.

By holding these materials in their hand, and thanks to the sensory experience of "touching" the numbers, kids learn first to associate something physical to the concept of numbers before going a step further in the abstraction process and associate them with numerical symbols.

Golden beads are just one of the materials used, there are many more, and they are usually so interesting for kids that their exposure to math through play/activity is very natural from the start.

If your child is attending a Montessori school, then you already know that it is suggested to avoid having at home the same materials available in class.

In any case, you can promote activities to support math learning. They have not to be complicated. For example, when in the kitchen, you could ask, "Would you be able to give me 3 spoons from that cutler tray?" or "We should beat 2 eggs to make a crêpe".

Have a look at Chapter 8 in this book for many ideas.

# SENSITIVE PERIODS – QUICK RECAP

♡ They are **phases** where the child instinctively moves towards a well-defined kind of experience, which allows him to **grow intellectually and physically**.

♡ They are essential and necessary to help kids acquire specific **abilities and traits** crucial for their development and well-being. They are:

♡ **Movement and coordination**

♡ **Sensory awareness and exploration**

♡ **Language**

♡ **Sense of order**

♡ **Social skills and good manners**

♡ **Music**

♡ **Writing**

♡ **Reading**

♡ **Mathematics**

# CHAPTER 2

# THE "ABSORBENT MIND"

"There is in the child a special kind of sensitivity which leads him to absorb everything about him, and it is this work of observing and absorbing that alone enables him to adapt himself to life. He does it in virtue of an unconscious power that only exists in childhood."

— Maria Montessori

**M**aria Montessori believed that even though a kid cannot talk before the age of 1 year or longer, it does not mean that he is not learning anything. In fact, a young child's mind can absorb knowledge exposed to them and has the power to teach themselves, despite not being able to speak. This is what Maria Montessori refers to as the kid's "absorbent mind," which is 'at work' during the first six years of life.

The absorbent mind presents two phases: an unconscious one, from birth to 3 years old, and a conscious one, from 3 to 6 years old.

During the first phase, the child "learns everything without knowing he is learning it, and in doing so, he shifts little by little from the unconscious to the conscious."

By this, Montessori means that until three years, the kid can learn simply by absorbing everything that they hear around them into their unconscious mind, quickly and effortlessly.

"The things he sees are not just remembered; they form a part of his soul."

— Maria Montessori

The child does not just learn the words of the language; he understands the sentence structures as well. This explains why we can speak our mother tongue very well: it is a language we learn during our infancy.

If we want a child to learn a specific language, we can immerse them in an environment where the language is frequently used. This piece of information will be stored until the kid is ready to make use of it.

This unconscious phase of the Absorbent Mind will stay with the kid until he is about three years old. After this, nature will decide when he will be able to use the information in his conscious mind. Slowly, the kid will establish memory, develop the power to understand and acquire reason. When these skills are fully achieved, the conscious mind will take over from the unconscious mind, and the child will start to become aware of what they are learning. Nobody can have any control over when such a transition will take place because "children grow according to natural laws."

# THE ABSORBENT MIND – QUICK RECAP

♡ It is 'at work' during the **first six years of life** of the child.

♡ It presents **two different phases**:

♡ an **unconscious** one, from birth to 3 years old: the child **learns by absorbing** everything that they hear around, quickly and effortlessly.

♡ a **conscious** one, from 3 to 6 years old: the child establishes memory, **develop the power to understand,** and acquire the ability to reason.

# CHAPTER 3

# BASIC PRINCIPLES

"Our care of the child should be governed, not by the desire to make him learn things, but by the endeavor always to keep burning within him that light which is called intelligence."

— Maria Montessori

In this Chapter, we will see the Montessori method's essential principles starting from the one around which the method itself is built: teaching children to be autonomous.

Let me tell you immediately that this will be a point where you will spend quite some time and will probably give you some headaches. Especially if you are used to moving fast and have to train your patience to manage daily tasks with kids constantly. But the good news is: you and your children will learn a lot, and with some tips we will see in the next Chapter, you will admit that it will be totally worth it.

Let me give you some examples.

Toddlers are messy eaters, and it generally means stained clothes, dirty floors, counters, chairs, and so on. Many parents feed their children rather than deal with the mess. This is precisely the opposite of what your child needs to develop their skills and learn to be independent. So, deal with the mess. Show them a few times the best way to eat, then accept there will be spills and food all around and allow them to feed themselves.

Another point where us parents usually fail to apply Montessori's principle of independence: dressing time.

Kids often express their personalities through their clothing. If you want them to be independent, allow them to get dressed by choosing clothes by themselves. They will sometimes arrange some creative outfits, but as long as clothes are suitable for the season (and this is a point you can easily manage), it's okay.

Children desire to be competent and master as much of themselves and their environment as possible. Suppose you devote time and effort to teach them independence by showing them how to perform every task. In that case, they will typically learn to do things with great concentration, interest, and evident satisfaction.

The younger the child, the better.

Allow ample time to the process and do one thing at a time, until the child absorbed the way to do it. Whether it's to wash hands, button a shirt, or set the table, proceed slowly, so that the child can try to replicate each step. An autonomous child is a confident child.

# EVERY CHILD IS DIFFERENT

Maria Montessori cherished children in their uniqueness. Her method keeps into high consideration that every child is different and that it's what makes a child unique, rather than what makes them ordinary to be important. For her, art was a tool to exploit children's creativity and individuality and express them even before acquiring the language.

Each child is also different in their time of learning things and acquiring skills, and it's imperative to meet their needs and don't force them.

# REPETITION IS KEY

Kids learn by doing, and repetition is how they concentrate on their tasks and master new skills. While they are in this process, it's essential to observe and do not interrupt, so that their attention can be on what they are doing at 100%.

Children observe their environment; they formulate hypotheses and test them by carrying out experiments.

Not sure about what this means?

A toddler throwing objects from a high chair isn't doing it out of malice. It's part of learning what happens if you drop different sized items from a height or what happens if you apply some force behind the objects and throw them.

Children learn through direct experience and repetition, and as parents, we should do our best to support this process.

# ENCOURAGE CHILD'S CURIOSITY

Curiosity in children comes in many forms. When they are younger, they explore as much as they can. When they can talk and interact with adults, a never-ending sequence of "Why?" is not only typical but also very healthy for them.

I perfectly understand that after the 10th "Why?" you may be tempted to shout it down quickly. But we would be making a big mistake to trade this peace of mind with a kid who does not ask questions.

Curiosity about the world is a sign that our children are alive, continually learning, and growing to be the adults they are supposed to be. Observing things around them and wanting to know more about what is happening will help them to be successful in school and life in general.

# DON'T HELP AND DON'T FIX

"Never help a child with a task at which he feels he can succeed."

— Maria Montessori

Help is something that we, as parents, are always ready to give no matter what. Either we always had help as kids ourselves, or we didn't, and we struggled; it's a perfectly normal instinct. But is it ever useful?

Maria Montessori, who was a mother herself and, as explained in the Introduction, devoted part of her time in educating mentally disabled children, thinks not.

Children need space to try again and again to do different things. As long as they do not harm themselves in any way, it's okay. We can provide them with several appropriated materials and toys, but experiences involve not only play and education but also real-life tasks.

A child should be helped only if, after several attempts, they seem to have hit a roadblock and cannot complete their task. Task completion is essential for the child. A little support now and then, only when required, is the best way to help him experience things and boost his self–confidence.

Help should be granted with little/no words and introduced gently with words like *"Can I help you?"* + the action required to move forward.

We can also try giving little suggestions like *"Did you try turning it upside down?"*, *"Did you try removing the lid?"*

It's also imperative to avoid fixing their imperfections. For example, if your kid is learning to make their bed in the morning, accept that the sheets may not be perfectly folded.

The activity is much more important than the result, and repetition will help fix all the details.

# MISTAKES LEAD TO LEARNING

I don't know about you, but mistakes were demonized by my parents when I was a kid, and I actually had problems doing things in my life because I was too worried to fail. Knowing the Montessori method and point of view helped me manage the approach to mistakes and finally see them for what they are: the way to learn new things. Mistakes are an essential part of growth, Montessori says. Punish mistakes can have a tragic impact on the child, preventing his evolution.

When mistakes happen, the most intelligent and healthy thing to do is finding a way to go past it once the child calmed down and is ready to listen.

First of all, the child needs to listen to a description of what happened from a calm, neutral voice. Anger leads to anxiety and fear, which are not the best emotional statuses to improve.

Whether the child is younger or older, it's always possible to stimulate a discussion about what happened.

The child may not be aware of why it happened, but it's okay. The crucial point is understanding how to amend the mistake.

I know it's not easy sometimes to stay calm, but we as parents should always try to do our best about this.

Actually, after some time applying this approach, it should become more manageable because, in the end, rules are quite simple: did you break granny's vase? Pick up the broom and pick the pieces up. Did you spill the milk on the table? Get a cloth and clean. Did you had a fight with a friend, and maybe you pushed him and hurt him? When the friend is ready, go to him/her and say you're sorry. Hug him/her if you are allowed.

Family, in this case, leads by example. If everyone is used to accepts others' faults and move on, the child will have little to no problem adapting to Montessori's method.

Otherwise, it will probably take a bit more time, but it will improve all the family.

One last thing, dedicated to parents.

Our children are perfect at "being kids" and doing "kid things." What those "kid things" are, depends on them. I find that sometimes parents (and other grownups that look after kids) are worried because the kids are NOT good at being like them, or them when they were kids, or how they'd like kids to be, etc.

Just let kids be as they are, without comparisons, and embrace the journey with all its flaws. You will soon assist the miracle of their precious growth into well-balanced adults.

# OBSERVE AND AVOID JUDGMENT

"The task of the educator lies in seeing that the child does not confound good with immobility and evil with activity."

— Maria Montessori

Parents, caregivers, and educators have a well-defined role in Montessori's method: they are observators.

It seems very easy, yet it's something that usually has to be trained a bit. Not only do the parents have to limit themselves to observation, but they also have to avoid judgment. Sometimes children behave in a way we don't get.

Their instinct and personality guide them, so, as long as they don't hurt themselves, others or break things, it's okay. We support and appreciate them regardless of any behavior that may seem "strange" to us.

# GIVE THEM ROOTS AND WINGS

"The greatest gifts we can give our children are the roots of responsibility and the wings of independence."

— Maria Montessori

As parents, our goal is to assist kids in becoming responsible, self-reliant, independent problem solvers. This goes well beyond mere obedience to keep parents happy.

The ultimate goal is that children act responsibly because they learned it pays off, and it is in their own best interests. Using the strategies outlined in this book will help give your kids both roots and wings. You will allow them enough freedom to grow, expand their potential, and become responsible kids, with less stress and enjoyment for everyone involved.

It's crucial to create a structured, firm, and consistent environment to raise our children to reach this goal.

A few well-defined rules clearly stated, and no doubts about boundaries and consequences, doing something wrong, are all children need.

Without rules, it would be like asking our children to walk across a suspension bridge with no guardrails. What would this feel like for them? They would experience fear and worry, for sure. Providing those guardrails, we are providing safety, security, and stability.

The sense of safety is one of the basic needs of human beings, and children, of course, make no exception.

Use simple words to state the rules to be crystal clear for everyone, discuss them (don't impose them), and hang them where they are well visible to everyone as a reminder.

# RESPECT SELF-REGULATION

The Montessori approach simplifies disciplining your kids and cultivating a sense of responsibility in them, as it eliminates issues and distress tied to traditional parenting methodologies. This is possible thanks to her vision of the kid and, in particular, to another fundamental principle, which is: let kids mature self-regulation and then respect it.

Self-regulation is related to an individual's ability to plan, guide, and monitor their behavior internally. It is very complicated as it involves higher mental functions that occur within the maturing brain. To make an example, self-regulation works like a thermostat.

A thermostat measures temperature and compares the reading to the desired temperature preset by the operator. When the reading is over the threshold, the thermostat turns either a heating or cooling system on or off. Kids have to learn where the threshold is set for them.

Traditional parenting approaches do not consider self-regulation. Instead, children are forced to obey through talks, rewards, and punishments. This is precisely the opposite as Montessori aims for cooperation.

Forcing something on someone just creates temporary results. The irony of this manipulating behavior is that the more you use to control kids, the less influence you exert, weakening your relationship with them.

Manipulation leads to resentment, while real responsibility that comes from self-regulation means behaving appropriately because kids want to, not because they have to.

# EMPOWER WITH RESPONSIBILITY

When kids know that others are counting on them, and particularly when they show attachment to the adult expressing the request, there is a great incentive to carry through with it. Kids don't want to let down others they care about and want to be considered someone who can be counted on. Having kids be responsible for something, such as a family task, can significantly affect responsibility.

The task can be small or large, anything from filling the cat's bowl to set the table for young kids to mowing the yard or sweeping the driveway. Let the kid know you depend on them to follow through with this task because doing it benefits the entire family.

Everyone likes being in charge of something, and children, in particular, need to feel that something is within their control. Therefore, if you want your kids to exhibit responsible behavior, put them in charge of the exact behavior you want them to display.

For example, suppose you have a child who is always getting up from the table during important family dinners, the very few where you want everyone to be together from the beginning to the end. In this case, think of your child's exact opposite behavior and put her in charge of that responsibility. You could say, "*Julia, you are in charge of a very important task. I need you to keep all members of the family seated during dinner. Can you do this?*"

When put in control of something, kids will always perform the appropriate behavior because incongruity is very difficult for young people.

# BASIC PRINCIPLES — QUICK RECAP

♡ The Montessori method's essential principle is: **teaching children to be autonomous**.

♡ Every child is **different**

♡ **Repetition** is key

♡ Encourage the child's **curiosity**

♡ **Don't help** and don't fix

♡ **Mistakes** lead to learning

♡ **Observe** and avoid judgment

♡ Give them **roots and wings**

♡ Respect **self-regulation**

♡ Empower with **responsibility**

# CHAPTER 4

# MONTESSORI HOME

"The environment must be rich in motives which lend interest to activity and invite the child to conduct his own experiences."

— Maria Montessori

I n this Chapter, I will explain how to apply Montessori principles to your home to make it "Montessori-compliant" as much as possible. In our case, the Montessori approach really helped us create an environment where our children could finally thrive, with less chaos and more harmony.

I am firmly convinced that every family should look at these critical, yet simple suggestions.

It would be immediately clear that modifying the environment to adapt to children's needs is not difficult, and most of all, it doesn't necessarily require a lot of space or a lot of money.

Each family could (and should) start from what they have and adapt the theory to their situation.

And once again, listening to our children is very important. You will see that the new setting will require them to adapt, and most probably, you will notice a few changes to make things even easier. If the kid cannot complete all his tasks by himself after showing him what to do and allowing enough time to try again and again, you may probably have to change the position of some items or simplify things even more.

Just observe (and listen), and it will soon be clear.

If you use bins for toys, for example, ask your kid to show you how to put the toys away, sometimes something as simple as struggling to get the lid off is enough to deter the kids from actually doing their job. So next time your child isn't doing as you ask, take a step back and see if there is a physical reason why.

In a family, each member contributes according to one's abilities and age. In a Montessori approach, this translates into giving each family member the tools and resources to do things for themselves, and not dependent on others.

Independence and decision making can (and should) begin at a very young age. So, yes, there will be less "Moooooom!!!" shouted from one side of the house to the other, I promise.

Now, let's start analyzing the home, room by room, and understanding how to order/re-arrange items for the better.

Remember that everything needs to have its place in every room, and everyone in the family has to be encouraged to know where things are.

# HALLWAY

Leaving home is always a delicate phase that initially seems to require forever to complete, especially if there is more than one child. Winter (or rainy) days, in particular, with all the gear to put on and zips to close, are quite challenging for the child. My suggestion is that both the environment and the clothes are chosen wisely, especially if they are very young.

How is structured a hallway which allows kids to prepare themselves to go out? Well, that's quite simple.

The first thing kids usually do is putting shoes on, so a bench, a small chair, or a footstool will be perfect for sitting and doing it.

If there is more than one child and there is enough space, I recommend having a bench. Otherwise, a couple of stackable stools will be okay. Just be sure to find a model that is light and easy to move.

If you have space just for one stool, maybe the same you use in other house rooms, it's perfectly okay. And if you have more than one child, they will also experiment with what it means to wait for their turn.

So, which are the main tasks to complete in this case?

♡ Put shoes on or put them away

♡ Depending on the weather, put on or take off the jacket and hang it (teach them the Montessori coat flip – see table)

♡ Depending on the weather, put on or take off mittens, hats, scarves, etc.

♡ Take the backpack or put it away

Everyone should have their place to hang the jacket, leave the shoes, and all winter gear. So identify with the kid the correct area assigned to them. For the gear, in my house, everyone has a cloth bag with lovely colors and patterns to hang it over the jacket, but you could give your child a box or a basket, which is 100% Montessori.

Providing a mirror would also be great to help them while they dress, but it's not essential.

---

# MONTESSORI

# 3 STEPS COAT FLIP

**1.** Coat tag to your toes

**2.** Your hands in the armholes

**3.** Flip the coat over your head

♡ **DONE!** ♡

---

# BEDROOM

The child's bedroom is one of the most important rooms in the house, so I suggest spending some time to optimize each detail, following the child's needs as they grow.

Let's start from the bed.

There are many solutions available on the market, and I suggest two: the first is putting the mattress on the floor, over a flat weave carpet. It will be effortless to clean, and your child will be able to sleep in their bed very early without the risk of falling.

An alternative is a shallow bed, preferably made of wood. It has to be possible to climb up without effort.

Let's now have a look at the closet and at the process to dress up in the morning.

A low clothes rod and low pegs in your kid's closet will make it possible to choose the clothes to wear, which is an activity that soon develops a great sense of pride and competency. Clothes should be ordered so that it's easy to find everything. I suggest making it available just clothes for the current season, to avoid morning tantrums because the child wants to wear some beachwear in winter (I've been there!).

Please note that also shelves or drawers are okay, as long as the child can reach them.  If not, it will be enough to provide a stool.

Once the child is old enough (my suggestion: asap!), we will teach them how to fold clothes and put them away, maybe following the effortless Marie Kondō folding style (Have a look at "The Life-Changing Magic of Tidying Up:

The Japanese Art of Decluttering and Organizing" by Marie Kondō)

A mirror will be a big help in learning how to dress up quickly.

If the bedroom is shared with other brothers or sisters, everyone must have their place. Decorate each space differently, following each child's taste.

If you have a toy room, then don't add much more to that and leave the bedroom as a place to sleep and dress up for the day.

If you don't, just apply the suggestion in the next paragraph to the bedroom or other house areas you want to dedicate to your child's play, activities, and reading.

# TOY ROOM

Toy room, or toys in general, are a subject around which there are many discussions.

On average, in non-Montessori environments, children just "have too much." The space dedicated to playing is so full of things that it becomes harder to play. It's a paradox that perfectly describes how children's minds work. Too many stimuli at a time, and there's a shutdown.

Luckily, this situation is relatively easy to solve. It will require some time and patience, but your kid will guide you, and like many things you will try after reading this book, it will be worth it.

The first thing to do is to check the toys and make an inventory. For me, it worked best without kids around, to avoid objections. Did you notice that a child might be interested in a toy if you told him you're going to donate it? They don't like change, and that is a change for sure.

Set aside the toys that haven't been used for a while and leave the others.

Once you have this subset, use boxes or baskets to order them and check that all the pieces are available. If not, set the toy aside. Also, a tip I always suggest in this phase is mark items that should be kept together with bright-colored tape bits. For instance, all the pieces of one puzzle can be identified with red tape on the back, etc.

You should end this selection process having sorted several toys, and maybe they are still too much to be ordered in the space available.

In this case, select some of them and put the rest away, so that you can rotate them now and then, creating new interest in the child.

As you finish this work of selection, as usual, observe. Children love repetition, and depending on how much time yours can dedicate to play, one or two weeks should be enough to identify their favorites and the ones they never use.

Put them aside and replace them with others. If they are in good condition, you may evaluate to donate them or sell them. Your kids are not using them anyway, and less stuff around is usually better for everyone.

In the last Chapter of this book, I will put a list of Montessori toys and non-Montessori toys that can adapt beautifully to this approach.

Keep toys on low, open shelves where they can be reached easily. Each one should have its specific location to encourage your kid to return it to the same spot before he begins playing with something else.

The toy room should have an area dedicated to reading, a cozy spot with some pillows on the ground, and a low library with a few selected books will be the perfect option. My younger girl asked to set up her reading room in a princess castle, so we did. We bought a tent with a castle on it, and she moved her pillows and books inside. But we could have done it in several other ways, with DIY... if we were DIY people (unfortunately, we are not, haha!).

Of course, a more standard table and chair would do.

If you have more than one child, you could consider moving the reading spot so that the child wanting to read is not disturbed by the others playing. Of course, we teach our kids to respect others' privacy, but sometimes this just doesn't happen, especially with very young siblings around.

Same considerations here as we did for toys. Too many books are not easy to manage. It's better to choose a few and rotate them now and then. Books should be displayed showing their beautiful covers, to encourage children to read them.

Toys and books are shared, and children must learn to wait for their turn, manage frustration, and move autonomously to another activity if they don't want to wait.

# BATHROOM

The bathroom is the room that is usually "almost Montessori" since the beginning. Kids love water and love learning how to clean themselves.

Once the child is old enough to use the toilet, be sure to leave a stool handy to climb on and be autonomous.

The stool is also essential to reach the sink, where they will find soap, toothbrush, and toothpaste.

Their towels will be hanging from a low wall hook or towel holder.

I also arranged a 3-tier rolling bathroom cart where I put some toiletries and some toilet paper. It took me some time, but now my kids change the empty roll by themselves.

What I suggest here, as always, is to observe your child. Some kids, my youngest for sure, is very attracted by toilet rolls (she like to play with them) and liquid soap or shampoo. It took me some time before finding the right bathroom setup, which was good enough to allow her to do things without me and prevent a total mess with every visit to the bathroom. In a blink of an eye, she was older and not attracted by those things anymore.

# KITCHEN

Maria Montessori insisted on making children independent in every field, even when that means to let them use objects that can be broken, like plates or glasses. Of course, adult supervision is always required, especially at a very young age, but at the same time, kids learn quickly that using two hands to bring glasses or plates means having better control.

We let our kids put some dishes, cups, and silverware on a low shelf to set their place at the table. We selected very cheap items so that I wouldn't have been a problem if someone dropped one. The thing is, so far, I broke many more glasses than my kids did, haha!

I tell you this because sometimes we tend to ask ourselves: "Isn't too much to let my child do this?" The answer is "No." most of the times. Our children are ready to learn well before we are prepared to let them do it. But luckily, we can work on it and do the best for them.

Under supervision, children should start cutting their food too. Of course, this means starting from an effortless task like cutting a banana with a butter knife.

It is also very useful to have a high stool (the IKEA one with two steps is perfect!) or a Montessori learning tower to help the child help while cooking.

Cooking is maybe the most important activity for the family, and involving our kids is unique both for them and us.

Now, I perfectly understand that we live hectic lives, and some days we hardly make it to the end of the day, but it's essential to find some time to cultivate the relationship with our children also through food. This is beneficial under so many points of view; for example, they learn the basics of healthy eating without effort. They learn to love the food they help to prepare. They manipulate ingredients, and this is a significant experience from a very young age.

There's never been any cooking tradition in my family. I have to thank Maria Montessori for this too. To be honest, I am not a great cook, but we have fun and build memories, which is invaluable to me.

Another plus is that kids love to clean, so my kitchen has a series of dish towels, kitchen paper towels, kitchen sponges, dish soap (with pump, to avoid excess use), a brush, and a dustpan. They are all well accessible to everyone so that whatever happens, we can help each other clean.

The last important point about the kitchen is leaving water and food available if the child is hungry. I suggest having a refillable water bottle, ecologic, straightforward to clean, and to refill. As far as food, it depends on the kid: some can control themselves and eat just enough to curb hunger. Others have no limit, so the best thing to do at the beginning is leaving a portion of whatever snack your kid is used to have and see what happens.

Observation will help you once again to understand what is best for your child.

## DINING ROOM

The dining room is elementary, as children's main task is to set up the table and clean it after lunch/ dinner. When they are very young, you could evaluate using placemats instead of a standard tablecloth as they are much easier to set up and put away.

## LIVING ROOM

I left the living room as the last room of the house to talk about because I wanted to demonstrate first how the rest of the house can be easily child-friendly. When all the other rooms are set up, you will see that your kids will appreciate their spaces and use them better than before.

I am genuinely convinced that parents, too, need a room for themselves, and that cannot be just the bedroom because being a family also means having social occasions. In my house, the living room is the space that is always ready to enjoy this kind of circumstances, and this means that it is usually toy-free and in perfect order.

I am not saying that kids cannot enjoy this space, too, because they do. But I also believe in balance and deprive parents of their needs has a huge toll. I used to be worried about guests coming; now it's much better. Everyone has their space, including mom and dad.

As far as the furniture, mine was already minimal, so I didn't do any particular change. What I did was removing the most fragile ornaments, but I could put them back to their place almost immediately as my kids have never been interested in them.

# MONTESSORI HOME — QUICK RECAP

♡ Start from what you have and adapt the theory to your situation.

## ♡ HALLWAY

Put **shoes** on / put them away:  **a bench**, a small chair, or a footstool.

Put on or take off the **coat** and hang it: **individual peg**.

Put on or take off **mittens, hats, scarves**, etc.: **individual basket/box/bag**.

Take the **backpack** or put it away: **dedicated place**.

## ♡ BEDROOM

A **mattress on the floor**, over a flat weave carpet or **shallow bed**, to climb up without effort.

A **low clothes rod** and **low pegs** in the closet.

If multiple children, **private space for each one**.

## ♡ TOYS ROOM

**Less is more. Select** some toys and put the rest away, so that you can **rotate** them.

Keep toys on **low, open shelves** where they can be reached easily, each with its specific location.

Add an area dedicated to **reading.**

## ♡ BATHROOM

**Stool** to use the toilet and reach the sink, with soap, toothbrush, and toothpaste.

Towels hanging from a low wall hook or towel holder.

## ♡ KITCHEN

Let them use objects that can be broken, like **plates or glasses.**

**High stool or learning tower** to let the child assist and help while cooking.

Dish towels, kitchen paper towel, kitchen sponges, dish soap (with pump, to avoid excess use), brush, and dustpan for the child to **clean.**

**Water and food available** in case the child is hungry: refillable water bottle and snack.

## ♡ DINING ROOM

**Set up the table** and clean it after lunch/ dinner.

Evaluate using placemats instead of a standard tablecloth.

## ♡ LIVING ROOM

Everyone has their space, including mom and dad, to have **social occasions** in an adequate area.

Minimal furniture, **remove** fragile ornaments.

# CHAPTER 5
# DAILY ROUTINES

"The essence of independence is to be able to do something for one's self."

— Maria Montessori

C hildren love order, security, and predictability, and routines are the best tools to ensure them. When a routine is in place, your kid knows when they will be having breakfast, lunch, or dinner; when it is playtime; when it is time for a bath and time to brush their teeth; they know when it is time to go to bed or to clean their room. Routines are strongly recommended when following the Montessori method at home.

They can be incredibly beneficial: they make family life more straightforward while teaching your toddler new skills and building self-confidence. Your children will know what to expect, which will create less stress in their lives, resulting in better behavior and attitude. They will be able to learn the satisfaction of 'a job-well-done' as they complete everyday tasks autonomously, without having to be encouraged or scolded or begged.

Ideally, many moments and activities can be set up in routines, especially during days with a similar structure (e.g., workdays may be different from weekends).

Divide the day into sections: every section can have its routine. Then, discuss each one with your children.

Involve them, describing the actions required, and all the steps from start to finish with a few exact words. Without a proper explanation, routines will not be effective. So, speak slowly as your kid, especially if very young, may not have any idea of what you are talking about and need to visualize the context and the actions. A suitable method is to print some images related to the routine steps, discuss them with the child and hang them to see them whenever needed.

It will take some time to learn all the steps of the process and remember what comes next, just be patient, and look at the big picture.

What works like a charm in my house is associating a "password" to each routine. It adds fun, and my kids know that when mom calls "monster's bedtime!" we will prepare us for the night.

Another suggestion is to do a quick check on your kids BEFORE you call for a routine. If your kid is doing some kind of activity and concentrating on it, if possible, do not interrupt. If the activity seems to be very long, announce you will stop it in 10 minutes, and they will finish it tomorrow. The interruption will not be a surprise, and you should avoid tantrums. Especially if the kid is very young, this is important as interruptions (and changes in general) until a certain age – different for every kid – are not very welcome.

Remember that children live in the present; they do not have a clear idea of what "future" means. They may seem slow to us, but slowness is essential for them to process everything their minds are managing.

Often more time and practice are all they need, and the look of how proud they are after the achievement, however small, is worth every second we give them.

Of course, there will be crazy days with no time at all. In that case, it will be allowed to help your child to speed up gently. Remember them that you recognize their ability to complete the task by themselves, but unfortunately, time is almost up, and you need to go.

# MORNING ROUTINE

To start the day well, I suggest setting up a morning ritual where the child gets up, uses potty/toilet, has breakfast, brush teeth and hair, gets dressed, makes the bed, and goes to school. Of course, you can vary the type and the order of the activities to suit your family needs.

When children are very young, you have to practice each step with them, but as they grow, the routine will remain in place, and they will follow it every morning by themselves after they awaken.

To make the routine as smooth as possible, and avoid frustrations, do a quick check of what the child will need to follow it.

Is the potty available and clean?

If the child already uses the toilet, do they need a stool to get up?

If you keep it underneath the sink, is the child aware of this? Can they get it?

Are toothbrush, toothpaste, towels, and brush readily available? And what about clothes and shoes? Are they easy enough to put on?

How do you arrange breakfast? Are foods ready for the child to prepare on their plate or mug and eat?

Answering these questions will help you identify potential issues and solve them before they stop your child during the routine.

# NIGHT ROUTINE

If possible, the night routine is even more important than the morning one because both you and your children are tired after a day out and need to finally relax and enjoy some time together.

The routine will start right after dinner and include a bath, brushing teeth and hair, putting on pajamas, and reading/cuddling together. You may change the order of these tasks and also add others, like picking up toys.

Your child may need three or four calming activities that, repeated consistently, will become a cue and will make them understand when it's time to go to sleep.

## CHOOSE BEDTIME

It's essential to decide when bedtime is and try sticking to it as much as possible with very few exceptions.

After a short period, the child will be in the habit of doing these things each day, and they will become sleepy at this time.

You are training their internal clocks to need sleep at this time.

We all need a good night's sleep to achieve the best during the day. The Sleep Council defined the average hours of sleep based on age, and the results are as follows:

# AVERAGE HOURS OF SLEEP

- ♡ **Birth-1 year:** 14-15 hours per day
- ♡ **1-3 years:** 12-14 hours per day
- ♡ **3-6 years:** 10-12 hours per day
- ♡ **7-12 years:** 10-11 hours per day
- ♡ **12-18 years:** 8-9 hours per day
- ♡ **Adults:** 7-9 hours per day

Now that you know how much sleep your child needs every night, you will be able to create a healthy sleep schedule that will help them develop their memory, improve their overall mood, and perform better in school.

Make your child's room cool and comfortable. Try to keep the room dark with a soft nightlight. The temperature of the room should be around 65-67 °F. If you are going to read stories to your child, use a tableside lamp with a low wattage bulb.

## BATH TIME

Use warm water for their bath and try to use soap or shampoo with lavender. This will help calm and relax the child.

Before you bath your child, let them lay out the clothes they will be wearing to bed. They will get dressed faster after they are sleepy and cranky from the warm tub.

## TEETH BRUSHING

Children should start good oral hygiene at the earliest. Parents of infants should cleanse their mouths with a clean cloth after meals and before going to bed.

As soon as they grow enough, it's essential to teach them to brush their teeth by themselves, and this is relatively easy, as long as it's fun for them and is done through rhyme. Let your toddler know that there are germs that we can't see living on their teeth, and it's vital to get rid of them. You can even make a song about it and ask for the help of a stuffed animal they love to assist.

The first time, hold the child's toothbrush and show them the proper way to brush teeth. Once you have demonstrated the process, hand your child the toothbrush and let them try while you brush your teeth as well.

As we said previously, it's essential to use very few/no words while showing to keep them concentrated on what they are learning.

Be consistent and repeat the process several times a day, as you would typically do. At the beginning, you will brush teeth together, then you may just supervise while they do, and in the end, they will be able to do it by themselves.

Since it is a process that requires a few steps, it may be a good idea to put on the bathroom mirror a visual sequence that both the toddler and parent can check during tooth brushing. This will support them to understand better the skill they are mastering.

## STORYTIME

Sometimes children are overly excited about something, other times they are cranky because they are exhausted. Either way, storytime allows you and your child to unwind and relax. It's a precious time for both of you, a time for cuddling and bonding, which will create lasting memories.

Us parents are often so tired that we neglect this moment. I suggest to keep it a bit shorter, if needed, but to do our best to have it every day.

If there are more children in the same room, it will become magical. If every child has their room, it will be an occasion to dedicate some exclusive time, and the child will surely be glad to have mom or dad just for them.

Let the child pick the book. If it is too long, choose the section you're going to read and save the rest for the next day. The great thing about reading a book is that it allows the child to get comfortable and tell you if anything is wrong (itchy pajama tag, uneven blankets, missing a plush toy, etc.). When you are done reading, kiss your child goodnight, turn off the light, and close the door.

## TECHNOLOGY USE AND OTHER SUGGESTIONS

If you are already following a Montessori approach, I'm sure your children have not much access to technology. But this guide is for all parents, and electronic devices are widespread in most families.

Unfortunately, using technology devices before bed will cause difficulty in falling asleep. Several studies say that after 1.5 hours of looking at a screen, our body decreases melatonin production. Melatonin is the hormone that induces sleep.

This is why children should limit technology such as television, video games, cell phones, and computers, especially before bed. Instead, encourage other activities such as reading, drawing, or playing. As a parent, even you should respect this good habit, because your children follow your steps.

Pay also attention to foods and drinks. Fatty foods, sugary snacks, and soft drinks are not healthy and consumed before bedtime can confuse your child's body and steal his sleep while healthy eating has been proven to promote quality sleep. Besides, feed your child at least 2 hours before bedtime. This can help your child establishing healthy eating habits too.

# EATING ROUTINE

If there's a time that we love the most, even during working days, it's mealtime because it allows us to share some precious time together, and gives us the opportunity to learn something new about our kids and vice-versa.

I am writing at the end of the summer of 2020, and this year will be remembered for the spreading of Covid-19, which caused so much trouble all around the world.

Well, I must say I like to find positive in everything, and for sure, being quarantined at home during lockdown has made us appreciate this time together even more.

If before Covid-19, eating all together was something we could rarely do because of crazy hours, our jobs, and children's activities, it has become a staple, and it probably has for your family too.

Now, let's talk about the eating routine. By that, I mean all the tasks related to preparing/cleaning the table, cooking food, and eating together. Depending on the day, kids can contribute in several ways to this critical moment of the day, so let's look at the tasks.

One of the main activities a child can learn to do is setting up the table for lunch and dinner. In the previous section, we discussed the characteristics a Montessori kitchen should have. It includes letting children manage plates, glasses, and cutlery stored on a shelf or other location easily accessible to the child. Show the child how to prepare the table and let them do it.

Cooking is something kids love to do, and sensory development through manipulating food is fantastic. You can start at a very young age. As long as they can sit, they can assist while mom cooks, and when growing up a bit, they can wash vegetables and fruit, measure and mix ingredients in a bowl, and many other activities that may be a little tricky and require supervision.

Following a nutritious diet is very important for children's health, and leading by example is, as usual, the best method to let them eating well. Involve them in cooking, including wholefood, colorful vegetables and fruits. You will see that kids will continue with this healthy routine, nearly instinctively, and everything you do will encourage them towards healthy eating habits.

Let them serve alone, but monitor them closely. Kids generally have much more control than we do because, essentially, they still have their natural hunger instinct. As parents, we should do everything to preserve it because it is essential to stay lean and healthy. Don't force them to eat everything if they are not hungry. If you are concerned about your child leaving some food behind, consider that the issue may be easily solved by preparing smaller servings. If your child tends to overeat, let them know the risks associated with overeating with simple words and keep a close eye on what they do. The observer role assigned to parents in the Montessori approach is essential to identify any issue in this field.

Mealtime becomes easier when planned in advance, and it's a pleasant experience to allow older kids to participate in programming. You can instruct them on preparing a perfect and well-balanced meal, using a book if needed to determine the foods they want to include. You will see that they will emulate what you already did for their meals since they were babies.

The last activity you can assign to your kids is cleaning up: washing and drying dirty plates, cutlery and pots (or load the dishwasher), cleaning table and countertops, sweeping the floor.

Splitting chores between all the family members, maybe with some nice music to make it fun, will help finish quicker, and the child will once again feel part of the family and very much needed.

# LAUNDRY ROUTINE AND OTHER CHORES

Laundry is a routine that toddlers love to assist with. It is fun and educational to help sort laundry, and it can be done in at least two ways: by type of clothing (one pile will be pants, another one will be socks, etc.) or by color.

Toddlers also love to put clothes into the washer, turn it on, and add the detergent. Then they can help to hang laundry or put it in the dryer. Get them small hangers so that they can easily manipulate their clothes.

Once the clothes are clean, the child can learn to sort the laundry, identify their clothes, fold them, and pair socks.

Chores are part of everyday life, and following a Montessori approach means to involve children in all house maintenance tasks from a young age. In this way, they normalize these activities and learn that their help within the family is essential and that maintaining a house in adequate conditions requires the support of every member of the family.

No one is disputing that one-on-one playtime with a parent is essential for a child's well-being and development. Still, it's good to know there are ways you can successfully incorporate playing with your child into your daily tasks so that you can get on with them while your child learns and is active alongside you.

# POTTY TRAINING ROUTINE

With weaning, potty training is one of the most significant transitions the child does, learning to finally use the toilet and leave diapers behind.

Many parents are often worried about this phase and transfer this sense of urge and anxiety to the child. Nothing can be more wrong than this.

As we already learned from a previous chapter, Montessori strongly believes in the child's ability to learn by constantly repeating and emulating adults.

This is fundamental when it comes to potty training. Let the toddler take the lead. If they don't show signs of being ready or have no interest in sitting on the potty, be patient. Let them follow you at the toilet every time you go, explain what is happening, and encourage them to emulate you by sitting on the potty. Never get angry if they don't follow your instructions because eventually, they will do it; it's just a matter of time.

Just build up this new habit gradually. Many illustrated books are very helpful in explaining the process. You may want to introduce them to the child and iterate some of the disadvantages of wearing diapers, such as being wet, smelly, etc. without being pushy. Choose beautifully colored pictures, comment on what you see, and give a solution to the problem.

My little one liked a book (Peek-a-Poo What's in Your Diaper? By Guido Van Genechten) showing a story of animals wearing diapers, with flaps to reveal the diaper content. We used to say *"Ooooh, poor piggy. Can you see his dirty diaper? It's so smelly! What could he do next time? Yes! Using the potty!"*. I am among the ones that had to wait until she was almost 3 years old, but at the same time, the day she decided to let go of the diaper, she did it for day and night, and we never had an incident after that. She was ready.

Make the moment fun, and if the child wants to bring a book or a toy, why not? Potty time should be a fun time!

One thing that also works is challenging children to show the other parent or a sibling their new ability. They are very proud to master new skills, and they will like to show them to others.

A way to make the process smoother and more pleasant is being flexible. As long as you abandon the idea that you need to accomplish this task by a specific time and allow the child to develop the skill at their own pace, you will be more relaxed, and things will get better.

Follow Maria Montessori and trust the child; everything will happen when it's time.

# DAILY ROUTINES — QUICK RECAP

Children love **order, security, and predictability,** and routines are the best tools to ensure them.

Print some **images related to the routine steps** and hang them where the child can see them.

Associating a "**password**" to each routine. It adds fun, and kids know exactly what to do when they hear them.

## ♡ MORNING ROUTINE

The child gets up, uses potty/toilet, has breakfast, brush teeth and hair, gets dressed, makes the bed, and goes to school (vary type and order of the activities to suit your family needs).

Is the **potty** available and clean? If the child already uses the **toilet**, do they need a **stool** to get up? If you keep it underneath the sink, is the child aware of this? Can they get it?

Are **toothbrush, toothpaste, towels, and brush** readily available?

And what about **clothes and shoes**? Are they easy enough to put on?

How do you arrange **breakfast**? Are foods ready for the child to prepare on his/her plate or mug and eat?

## ♡ NIGHT ROUTINE

Both you and your children are tired after a day out and need to finally relax and enjoy some time together.

**Sleep:** Decide when bedtime is and try sticking to it as much as possible with very few exceptions.

**Bath time:** Use warm water for their bath, let them lay out the clothes they will be wearing to bed.

**Teeth brushing**: teach them to brush their teeth by themselves through rhyme.

Put a visual sequence on the bathroom mirror.

**Storytime** allows the child to unwind and relax before sleep.

Let the child **pick the book**. If it is too long, choose the section you're going to read and save the rest for the next day. When you are done reading, kiss your child goodnight, turn off the light, and close the door.

Using technology devices before bed will cause difficulty in falling asleep. Children should **limit the use of technology,** and you, as a parent, should respect this good habit because your children are following your steps.

## ♡ EATING ROUTINE

It involves all the tasks related to **preparing/cleaning the table, cooking food,** and **eating together**.

Let children **manage plates, glasses, and cutlery** stored on a shelf or other location easily accessible to the child.

Show the child how to prepare the table and let them do it.

**Assist mom while cooking,** wash vegetables and fruit, measure and mix ingredients in a bowl, and many other activities that may be a little tricky and require supervision.

**Clean up:** washing and drying dirty plates, cutlery, and pots (or load the dishwasher), cleaning table and countertops, cleaning the floor.

**Splitting chores between all the family** members will help finish quicker, and the child will feel very much needed.

## ♡ LAUNDRY ROUTINE AND OTHER CHORES

Help **sort laundry** in two ways:  by type of clothing (one pile will be pants, another will be socks, etc.) or by color.

Toddlers also love to put clothes into the **washer**, turn it on, and add the detergent.

Then they can help to **hang laundry** or put it in the dryer. Get them small hangers so that they can easily manipulate their clothes.

Once the clothes are clean, the child can learn to **sort the laundry**, identify their clothes, fold them, and pair socks.

Chores are part of everyday life, and following a Montessori approach means to **involve children in all house maintenance tasks** from a young age.

In this way, they normalize these activities and learn that their help within the family is important.

## ♡ POTTY TRAINING ROUTINE

**Let the toddler take the lead.** If they don't show signs of being ready or have no interest in sitting on the potty, be patient.

**Let them follow you** at the toilet every time you go, explain what is happening, and encourage them to emulate you by sitting on the potty.

**Never get angry** if they don't follow your instructions.

Many illustrated **books** on the matter, pick one that gets your child's attention and read it repeatedly.

**Be flexible.**

Abandon the idea that you need to accomplish this task by a specific time and allow the child to develop the skill at his own pace, you will be more relaxed, and things will get better.

# CHAPTER 6

# PARENTS AND EDUCATION

"Scientific observation then has established that
education is not what the teacher gives; education is a
natural process spontaneously carried out by the human
individual, and is acquired not by listening to words but
by experiences upon the environment."
— Maria Montessori

M aria Montessori documented the influence of the
environment on children's development.
Education is not just what they learn at school,
but all the lessons they are unconsciously exposed since
birth. Parents are the most critical individuals that guide

kids to flourish and transform into the adults they will be in the future.

Leading by example since the very beginning, and reinforcing consistently the most important qualities, lessons and behaviors, they can become a successful role model, and their kids an example of respectful, independent, and better at making decisions human beings.

Children will carry these elements with them forever and use them to advance through life.

Today's world requires more than primary education. It rewards creativity, cooperation, the ability to put information together in new ways, curiosity, questioning, and asking difficult questions. Building close and collaborative interpersonal relationships is effortless when parents create the same sort of environment at home.

# RESPECT

"Children are human beings to whom respect is due, superior to us by reason of their innocence and of the greater possibilities of their future."

— Maria Montessori

In a Montessori home, like anywhere else, respect is both due and required. But unlike anywhere else, the child is considered at the same level as the adult, which means that their spaces, pace, and opinions are essential and respected.

This helps the child understand what respect means and what to do to be respectful of others.

In a well-balanced family, parents can teach respect in many ways. For example, fathers teach their kids to honor their mothers by honoring their spouses in the first place. Women teach their kids how to respect themselves by having a positive and healthy relationship with their husbands. When they disagree on something, trust leads to a solution. Trust is built over time, and like respect is at the base of everything, and it's a thing children learn from the beginning in a Montessori family.

Respect also means respect for others, and the children learn it inside the family too. For example, have you ever been to a restaurant and all you can hear are kids screaming?

Likely, the kids have not been taught the difference between an inside and an outside voice. This is a standard teaching for a Montessori family.

Outdoors is the place for speaking louder, but a quieter voice is required whenever indoors, and this concept, like all others, has to be communicated in the right way for the children to absorb it.

The right way to do it could be saying: "*We speak softly when we are inside*," with a gentle voice. Of course, repetition will be crucial, and the sooner you will start to introduce this concept, the better.

# PERSISTENCE

Persistence is an essential skill for everyone in everyday life. How many times does a situation develop precisely how we thought? Not so frequently.

This happens to children even more as their knowledge of the world is minimal and always growing. Montessori parents teach children to keep going, and this is the very foundation which allows us to remain strong amid crisis and adversity in adult life. Show your kids to never lose hope.

Help them overcome the frustration they will undoubtedly experience when trying to accomplish something, explaining that it's essential to keep calm and try again. Show them how to do it whenever possible, using as few words as possible.

Don't forget to reinforce their sense of achievement and share the excitement when they complete the task successfully.

## DISCIPLINE AND GOOD MANNERS

How parents interact between themselves and with others has a significant impact on children. In a loving, caring environment where all the voices matter and where even little one can express themselves freely, it's easier to develop discipline and good manners. Everyone counts, and their presence and contribution are very welcome. A child is an adult in development, and feeling accepted makes them feel worthy and willing to positively contribute to family tasks.

Calm and firm parents instill calm and collaboration in their kids. Of course, it's perfectly ok to lose patience from time to time. It happens to everyone, but making an effort to lead by example always pays off.

Teach your kids the best ways to interact with other children and adults and respect their environment. For example, show them how to greet someone when they meet them, practicing phrases like, *"Hello, nice to meet you!"*. Teach them to say, *"Please"* and *"Thank you."*

Teach them to dispose of trash in the proper bin and keep their room/space clean.

Teach them the "silence game" to learn to stay quiet and develop self-control.

Show them to ask for help without interrupting a conversation. In a Montessori environment, there is a signal to request attention: a gentle touch of the adult's shoulder.

These are just some ideas to teach "grace and courtesy" to say it with Maria Montessori's words.

# ♡ PRACTICE GOOD MANNERS ♡

♡ When you meet someone new, smile and introduce yourself. *"Hi, my name is Julia. Nice to meet you."*

♡ When someone introduces to you, say, *"Nice to meet you."*

♡ When someone is talking, listen and don't interrupt; when you are talking, require the same *"Please, I'm talking. Let me finish first"*.

♡ When you meet someone you know, say, *"Hello."*

♡ When someone leaves, say, *"Bye."*

♡ When you chew your food, your mouth is closed.

♡ When you see someone older than you, offer your seat.

♡ Dispose of your trash properly and recycle.

♡ When you need to apologize, say, *"I'm sorry."*

♡ Show kindness to all living things.

♡ When you cough, cover your mouth.

♡ When you sneeze, cover your nose.

♡ Wash your hands after the toilet.

# SELF-ESTEEM AND CONFIDENCE

Being able to approach various situations with confidence makes life much more pleasant, relaxed, and enjoyable - at work, social events, learning something new, or having time with family and friends. The skills needed to feel confident and independent can be taught to kids from a young age and will stay with them for a lifetime.

To build confidence, a parent can provide opportunities for their kids to do something successfully.

Putting effort into some kind of activity and being successful boosts confidence. The child starts thinking that if they can do that successfully, they can probably accomplish other things as well.

Building a kid's confidence also means doing their best to make them feel safe in their home assertive. They need to trust their judgments and think that they can easily make the right decisions independently.

Building confidence is about encouraging kids to feel good about themselves and their achievements. Following Maria Montessori's approach, avoid putting kids in positions of complete failure.

Create tasks that can be achieved through trial and repetition and make them achievable by giving appropriate support in exceptional cases that could lead to giving up. Increase the difficulty of the task as soon as the previous level has been mastered successfully. For example, if the task is a game where the child has to hit a ball with a racket, find a one so big and a ball so soft that success is inevitable. Once the kid can do this, make it more difficult - perhaps hitting the ball bouncing against a wall or using a smaller racket.

If the task is to encourage reading, make good books available, and if the kid struggles, read together until no more help is needed for them to succeed. Confidence will come as one small success builds on another.

More on this subject in the next Chapter.

# CURIOSITY

A curious mind learns to ask questions and is never tired of it. Through this method, a kid knows to find the answer independently, and Maria Montessori cherished this approach very much and recommended parents to do the same.

I say we should really encourage our kid's constant questions. It is OK – and perfectly normal – if we don't have all the answers: we can always learn new things by checking the solutions together or redirect our kid to find them elsewhere ("*Granpa should know this, you may want to ask him*").

Either way, we will improve our knowledge, stimulate the brain to create new connections (which is good for us too!), and teach our kids to persist until they satisfy their curiosity.

# SOCIAL SKILLS

Social skills are the ones we use every day to interact and communicate with others, and for this reason, they are a big step in every child's education. Skills like good manners and eye contact will help them make others feel comfortable with them and help them make friends. Modeling good manners and courteousness ourselves, we help our children develop vital strategies to succeed in their relationships. They will learn what to say and act in many situations, which will release anxiety and allow them to perform confidently.

Talk to your kids about why manners are essential and use examples to clarify your perspective. *"When your friend came over and didn't say hello to me, it hurt my feelings. Remember to always say hello when you go to someone's house."*

Practice good manners with your kids daily. This includes morning greetings, table manners, introducing friends and offering to help, etc. To help kids learn, as usual, use a straightforward language, they can quickly memorize.

If your child is old enough, use everyday situations to ask what they think about the behavior of the people around us. Is that child polite? Is that the way they should talk to their parent? Get your kid to think about how it could have been done differently.

Every social situation provides a teaching opportunity. Take a few minutes to prompt your kid. *"There is a new kid over there. How would you start a conversation with him?"* Your child has probably seen you many times introducing yourself to others and should be able to do it as well. Practice will make them confident.

# TANTRUMS MANAGEMENT

As parents, we know very well that, especially at a very young age, tantrums are perfectly normal, and they may happen for whatever reason, even in moments that seem to be very calm and relaxed.

A kid's brain is developing at the speed of light and is learning to process all the inputs received consciously and unconsciously. Sometimes things worsen, the mind is overflowing, and the child becomes angry, worried, emotional, or anxious.

We've all been there. Everything seems working like a charm; then our child starts screaming out of the blue, so loud that all people start staring at us and commenting with a complete lack of empathy.

Well, first of all, don't worry. Your kid will be okay, and you too. The most important thing now is to remember just one, super important detail: while the tantrum is ongoing, your child is completely absorbed in what is happening inside and cannot listen to you.

Did you notice that nothing works in these moments? Praise, threats, no words seem to catch their attention and cause a reaction.

So, **things to avoid** are: bits of advice, suggestions, and, most of all, questions! Urge them to reply in this moment will only cause the tantrum to get worse, as the child most probably doesn't know or can't retrieve in their mind the proper reply to your questions, causing frustration.

**Things to do immediately**: offer some tools to calm down. Are they a child needing contact? Offer some cuddles or a hug and do it gently, with a low voice and a few words as usual. Just ask *"Cuddles?"* or *"Can I hug you?"* and wait for them to show if it's ok. Some kids avoid contact, and in time you will learn what works best for them.

My eldest always appreciated cuddles, while the youngest prefers to have a quiet place where she can calm down by herself, knowing that mom is there just in case. Following Maria Montessori's lead, I always respected their requests.

From a physiological point of view, consider that hugs and cuddles release oxytocin, a powerful calming hormone, so I suggest going for it if your child allows you. Oh, and don't forget that us parents deserve some hugs for managing these difficult times successfully, too!

# PARENTS AUTO-OBSERVATION

Maria Montessori introduced a very powerful and, for the time, innovative concept: parents should regularly review their relationship with their kids and identify details that may be improved.

This is a difficult job for many reasons, the first is time, which seems always working against us, and it is also quite tough to evaluate things from the outside without letting emotions control us. Yet, I think that this is a critical task to repeat regularly. I don't have a particular schedule for this, but I do try to review the main problematic episodes that happen in my family and ask myself, *"What could I have done differently to manage that?"*.

I find that being so busy often makes me less patient and, even if I genuinely believe in Montessori's approach, it's still quite a challenge to go through some moments of epic mess. But the only way to improve ourselves and our parenting style is to always do our best and, of course, spend some time on training ourselves, again and again, to manage situations properly.

I find it a moment of growth as a couple because sometimes there is disagreement with my partner, and if we both want to put love first, we have to mediate, take a step back, and solve the matter.

I would like to give you food for thought. It's something I often think about, and I find it useful to find a way to simplify things.

When we interact with our children, which is the real reason behind what we ask? Are we asking to do specific tasks because they are needed or just because "it's always been like that"?

Where is our attention? On the completion of the task, following our way of doing things, or on the result, letting kids experiment their way?

I am asking this because I find myself replicating from time to time what I experienced myself as a child when I had to execute my mom's orders with no explanation attached ("do it like I say, just because I said it").

Sometimes, I find myself establishing too many rules than needed. And yes, Maria Montessori agreed about rules and limits appropriate for each kid's age, but they should only serve to educate them.

So, if you find yourself in the same situation as mine, LET IT GO! Don't overcomplicate your life and your children's.

A typical situation that used to stress me a lot was dinner time. In my house, we eat together every night and treasure this moment, trying to make the most of it.

Well, frequently, my children, especially the eldest, just didn't want to eat at the right time, saying she wasn't hungry.

I remember myself getting angry after several times in a row this happened. I totally lost the focus on the important thing: "my kid not being hungry" (kids won't let themselves starve to death, for sure!). One hour later, she would come to me asking for food. I remember replying something like, "If you have had eaten before, you wouldn't be hungry!". I lost again the focus on what was important: "my kid properly recognizing hunger signal and asking for food thanks to it" and also "the possibility for me to feed my kid properly," even if one hour later.

See? Who cares if rules are not correctly followed every time? Sometimes a bit of flexibility helps to stay focused on the most important things. The more we are locked into our way, the less control we can have over the outcome. And after all, that's the only thing we want to control.

Oh, and by the way, later on, I found out the reason why my daughter behaved like that: she found where granny kept sweets and had some without anyone noticing before leaving her house (so, yes, when she said, "I am not hungry," she really meant it).

# PARENTS AND EDUCATION – QUICK RECAP

Education is not just what they learn at school, but all the **lessons** they are **unconsciously exposed** since birth. Parents are the most critical individuals that guide kids to flourish and transform into the adults they will be in the future.

## ♡ RESPECT

Respect is both due and required. **The child is considered at the same level as the adult**, which means that their spaces, pace, and opinions are essential and respected.

Respect also means respect for others, and the children learn it inside the family.

## ♡ PERSISTENCE

Persistence is an essential skill for everyone in everyday life.

Montessori parents teach children to **keep going**, and this is the very foundation that allows remaining strong amid crisis and adversity in adult life.

## ♡ DISCIPLINE AND GOOD MANNERS

Teach your kids how to interact with other children and adults and respect their environment.

Show them how to greet someone when they meet him/her, practicing phrases like, *"Hello, nice to meet you!"*. Teach them to say, *"Please"* and *"Thank you."*

Teach them to **dispose of trash** in the proper bin and keep their room/space clean.

Teach them the **"silence game"** to learn to stay quiet and develop self-control.

Show them to ask for help without interrupting a conversation. In a Montessori environment, there is a signal, which is a **gentle touch of the adult's shoulder**, to request for attention.

## ♡ SELF-ESTEEM AND CONFIDENCE

Putting effort into some kind of activity and being successful will boost confidence because they feel they can do something right. The child will start thinking that **if they can do that successfully, they can probably accomplish other things as well**.

Create tasks that can be achieved through trial and repetition and make them achievable by giving appropriate support in exceptional cases that could lead to giving up.

## ♡ CURIOSITY

A curious mind learns to ask questions and is never tired of it; through this method, a kid learns to find the answer independently.

## ♡ SOCIAL SKILLS

Social skills are the ones we use every day to interact and communicate with others

**Modeling good manners** and courteousness ourselves, we help our children develop vital strategies to succeed in their relationships. They will learn what to say and act in many situations, which will **release anxiety** and allow them to **perform confidently**.

**Practice good manners with your kids daily**. This includes morning greetings, table manners, introducing friends and offering to help, etc. Use a **straightforward language** they can quickly memorize.

## ♡ TANTRUMS MANAGEMENT

A kid's brain is developing at the speed of light and is learning to process all the input received consciously and unconsciously. Sometimes things worsen, the mind is overflowing, and the child becomes angry, worried, emotional, and anxious.

So, **things to avoid** are bits of advice, suggestions, and, most of all, **questions**! Urge them to reply in this moment will only cause the tantrum to get worse, as the child most probably doesn't know or can't retrieve in their mind the proper reply to your questions, causing **frustration**.

**Things to do immediately**: offer some tools to **calm down**. Are they a child needing contact? Offer some **cuddles** or a **hug** and do it gently, with a low voice and a few words as usual. Just ask "Cuddles?" or "Can I hug you?" and wait for them to show if it's ok. Some kids avoid contact, and in time you will learn what works best for them.

## ♡ PARENTS AUTO-OBSERVATION

Parents should regularly **review** their relationship with their kids and identify details that may be improved.

*"What could I have done differently to manage that?"*.

When we interact with our children, **which is the real reason behind what we ask?** Are we asking to do specific tasks because they are needed or just because "it's always been like that"?

Learn to **let it go**. Don't overcomplicate your life and your children's.

# CHAPTER 7

# EFFECTIVE COMMUNICATION

The child has a different relation to his environment
from ours. The child absorbs it. The things he sees are not
just remembered; they form part of his soul.
He incarnates in himself all in the world about him that
his eyes see and his ears hear.
— Maria Montessori

As parents, we need to remind ourselves that our kids learn not only from what we say but by how we say it. Whether we always speak in anger, belittling others, or talk with openness and respect, our kids hear and emulate this. Despite this emulation ability, remember that children's cognitive skills are not yet fully developed. Depending on their age, they may be incapable of seeing another's point of view, perceiving all sides to a problem, or visualizing abstract concepts. So, it is essential to use an age-appropriate form of communication that shows that you understand their perspective and encourages them to voice their opinions when talking to them.

# EXCLUSIVE LISTENING

Being listened to is the first goal of communication from both sides, parents, and children. It leads to feeling validated, respected, and understood, but sometimes this just doesn't happen. Why?

Because exclusive listening, in today's world full of activities to do and distractions, is frequently ignored, but let me tell you there's no good communication between parents and children without it.

It's a matter of respect, a theme so dear to Maria Montessori, and it starts from us. Have you ever talked with your children when folding clothes, reading the newspaper, writing emails, or cooking meals? Then it's no surprise that sometimes, when we speak to them, their attention is not on the ongoing conversation or us at all. They are emulating. Add to the equation that, especially at a young age, they are easily distracted by the environment, and the result is that they don't listen.

This doesn't mean that you should stop doing whatever you are doing every time you need to talk to your children, but it's essential to dedicate your complete attention to them and total focus on the conversation every time you can. By making exclusive listening a priority, your kid will feel important and heard.

## MUTUAL RESPECT

By respecting our kid's needs and feelings, we will teach them, by example, how to respect us. We can show respect to our kids by accepting what they tell us as valid and vital. It is essential for our kid's self-confidence that we acknowledge their feelings and beliefs as real and authentic. We need to accept their vision and feelings, even when their perception of reality seems extorted.

Trying to understand things from their perspective, you will better understand the reasons causing their behavior. You will be able to provide alternatives and find solutions to issues, promoting a win-win situation for everyone.

For example, angry outbursts are often the result of built-up hurt or frustrated feelings. Taking the time to learn how our kids feel and see a particular event can help us resolve any underlying problem and tackle similar issues if they arise in the future.

It is essential to acknowledge the right to freely feel all kinds of emotions, with no need to stop expressing any. We should also help the child identify each sentiment by giving it a name and saying things like, *"I see you are very sad now."* This will help the child associate the feeling to the words to define it, and time after time, they will be able to express their emotions better.

We should let express and accept every emotion, as long as the child does not hurt himself or others or starts damaging things. In this case, we should gently stop them saying something that acknowledges their discomfort but also puts a limit to it. We could say:

*"I understand that you are very angry, but I have to stop you throwing books to your sister, or you are going to hurt her. Can I hug you now?".*

As you can see, in this phrase there are three main parts:

- ♡ We acknowledge the right to feel angry
- ♡ We say to stop positively (we avoid saying "don't" as children don't get negations)
- ♡ We offer a way to calm down (see the previous chapter for more alternatives)

# EYE CONTACT

Eye contact is crucial for kids, especially at a young age, so physically get down to their level every time you need to communicate with them, especially if it's a moment of exclusive communication with no interruption.

If we stand and talk over our kids, our words go straight over their heads. They are often unaware that we are talking to them; instead, our words are just background noise. Getting down to their level and making eye contact with them let them know you are talking to them, making it easier for them to listen and connect with you. You are also showing them respect by understanding and appreciating them for what they are.

## REPEAT WHAT YOU UNDERSTAND

Establishing good communication may be a challenging task for kids, especially when they are still very young. Concepts are not easy to think and express effectively, so parents have a significant role in validating their job and showing that their effort is appreciated. This will encourage them to communicate even more and consolidate their talking and reasoning skills.

You can help your children by repeating in your own words what you think they're saying and how they're feeling about it. You may say: *"You mean that…?"* or *"You seem sad now. Does it mean that you don't want to …?"*

Actively doing this gets you credit for understanding at both head and heart levels, which builds a robust and open relationship.

Show interest and use your voice and body to show that you listen, understand, care, love, and appreciate your children. You can do it in very subtle ways, like glancing sideways in the car, catching their eye, or turning towards them for a moment as you are in a supermarket's isles.

# KEEP IT SIMPLE

Children have many limitations on the way they can process what you say to them. For example, young kids simply do not understand things they cannot see, hear, or touch while older kids are still developing the ability to think in more abstract ways. In general, children are still very selfish in their thinking; that is, they see the world through their experiences and find it hard to take a third-person perspective.

Because of these limitations, when we communicate with them, we need to do it in a basic way. In other words, keep it simple and to the point. Use examples that children can relate to.

This is very useful, especially when we are outside, and we need to communicate tasks to execute immediately. Still, of course, it doesn't mean it has to be our only way of communicating. Language skills grow when children are exposed to a rich vocabulary from a very young age.

Let's just choose the best communication style in every situation.

# SUPPORT SELF-ESTEEM

As we told in the previous chapters, the words we use have a significant impact on our children, which is why we should think carefully before we speak.

Words can have a positive or negative tone. For example, compare *"You are always so clumsy!"* with *"You are very energetic!"*. Which sentence do you think will make your child feel good?

Uplifting words have the power to raise your kid's self-esteem, and we should always use them in our communication to consolidate it from a very young age.

Imagine your son is learning fractions. He goes, "I can't understand this, it's too hard. I always get it wrong."

Instead of replying an abrupt, "You're always so impatient. It takes time to learn something new." you could opt for a more reassuring, *"I know you have a quick mind. If you think about it a bit more, I'm sure you will soon understand it."* In this way, you are communicating your trust in his capabilities, and you will encourage him to try harder.

If your daughter drops a bottle of juice while she is helping you in the kitchen, avoid saying "You're so careless, why can't you do anything right?", which will turn her off from helping ever again, and opt for an encouraging *"Use the towel to mop up the juice. You are usually so cautious, what happened today?"*

We all like to hear things that make us feel good about ourselves. It is even more critical for kids because the words they hear daily are the words that shape their perception of who they are. If a child is encouraged and feels capable, they grow up to be optimistic and happy, naturally developing a feeling of worth and value.

On the other hand, if a child feels bad about themselves, it is tough to change that feeling growing up. They might feel unworthy though achieving great things.

Say something positive every day to those you love and see how much better they feel. Self-esteem is how we feel about ourselves, and our behavior reflects those feelings. If your kid has high self-esteem, they are likely to act independently, assume responsibility, take pride in their accomplishments, tolerate frustration, attempt new tasks and challenges, handle positive and negative emotions, and offer others assistance.

If your kid has low self-esteem, they will avoid trying new things, feel unloved and unwanted, blame others for their shortcomings. They will feel (or pretend to feel) emotionally indifferent, be unable to tolerate an average level of frustration, put down their talents and abilities, and be easily influenced.

Here some examples of affirmations I tend to include often in my communication with my daughters. They are straightforward, yet so powerful. You can think of yours and start practicing when talking to your kids.

*"You are independent and capable."*

*"You know what you want, and I love this."*

*"You are brave, and I believe in you."*

*"You always find ways to accomplish your goals."*

Of course, affirmations are very useful if practiced by kids too, and you could try concise ones (*"I am smart," "I am grateful," "I feel confident,"* etc.) and ask your child to repeat after you.

# DON'T PRAISE

Maria Montessori discouraged praise. In her vision, the child acts to develop their path, not to make us happy, not to get our approval. Praise by itself is useless. Punishment is useless, as well. A child shouldn't be forced to do something just because they fear our reaction.

When I was a child, praise was used very much (and to be honest, it still is at Granma's despite all my effort to explain, ha!). Growing up, I found it ingrained in my brain.

I trained a lot to remove it entirely, but sometimes it still pops out. Talking with other Montessori teachers many years ago, I learned an excellent way to combine it with words that describe the activity completed by the child. Praise will not be the main message the child will get and will just reinforce my approval.

For example – I put into brackets the part we should skip:

♡ *(Well done!) You drew a huge red circle!*

♡ *(Fantastic!) You put your dirty t-shirt in the washing machine!*

♡ *(Wow!) You filled the cat's water bowl!*

♡ *(Impressive!) You spilled the water and wiped it with a cloth!*

These are straightforward phrases, perfect for very young kids. As long as they grow up, I suggest expressing yourself with a bit more complex sentences, that are an occasion to improve the child's language as well, by associating abstract concepts to concrete actions. For example:

♡ *You used watercolors and then hanged your painting. You are very creative!*

♡ *I like it when you brush your teeth and put on your pajama all by yourself. You are so independent!*

♡ *I like the way you've chopped the tomatoes. You've been very helpful. What about cutting the zucchini too next time?* (I want to challenge my children, make them feel they are moving towards a higher goal and that I trust they have the skills to get there)

I find a very positive thing to let know my kids when I feel good thanks to them. Parents are sometimes quick to express negative feelings to kids, and it's ok; we are humans, and it happens. In this case, let's move on and spend some time to learn how to express our negative feelings correctly and train ourselves to describe positive feelings instead, whenever possible.

Kids don't know when we are feeling good about them unless we tell them. In this case, they store positive statements up and repeat them to themselves over and over again. Train yourself to look for situations where your kid is working hard to do a good job, facing a new challenge, overcoming a difficulty, and show your appreciation to them - with no praise if possible – following the easy rule above.

# MANAGE CONFLICTS

In every family, conflicts may arise in many occasions every day. We have an idea of something while our children have a totally different, or even opposite, one.

These moments are sometimes hard to manage if we do not train ourselves to do so correctly. This is what I ask myself in these cases:

♡ Is my child's idea somehow acceptable, even if very far from mine?

♡ Is it something worth spending time to mediate, teaching them how to find a solution by themselves?

These two basic questions let me filter significant matters. If my kid wants to put on a dirty shirt because it's his favorite, is there a real need to spend some time managing his fight against me wanting to put on a clean t-shirt, or is it better to let it go this time and concentrate on the next significant conflict that may arise?

I started doing so because with kids growing up, conflicts are very common, and I think it's not very wise to concentrate on each one when we can focus on the most important ones and let go of the others. Our energy may be a lot, but it's easily depleted when spent in little things of no importance.

The best way to solve a conflict in a Montessori way is to stimulate the kid to find a solution by themselves. We could say, *"I understand your position, but unfortunately, this is not possible. What do you think we can do to solve this?"*

This simple question with no further help or hint will stimulate reasoning and, most of the times leads to some kind of alternative that we can further discuss (and in that case, I ask myself the same fundamental questions I wrote before).

Learning to manage conflicts is very important for parents and children and has to be learned from a very young age. It's part of creating and maintaining healthy relationships both inside and outside the family and helps the kid grow.

## COMMUNICATION MISTAKES

A few common mistakes may cause children to feel bad about themselves and not properly aiding their healthy growth. The words we say and how we say them will influence not just their present but, most importantly, their future, and that's why I am taking one more occasion to recall Montessori's concept of respect due at all ages.

Not only some approaches do not respect our children, but they also undermine their confidence and cause much damage to their self-image.

## WRONG LANGUAGE PATTERNS

Most damaging language patterns include words like: always, never, every time, all, etc. They state something which seems universally and unconditionally true, and this is a big problem.

The issue should be described as it is here and now. We don't know if it will happen again in the future. Our communication goal to the kid should always be to analyze what happened to avoid it in the future.

An example, look at the difference between the sentences:

- ♡ *"You never eat when it's time."* Instead, you could say: *"Yesterday you didn't eat with us either, are you not hungry now?"*
- ♡ *"You are mean and never show me respect"* You could say instead: *"You hurt my feelings, and I don't want you to treat me like that."*

Another wrong pattern is talking about the identity of the child in general rather the behavior, action or words, etc. that are currently problematic like:

- ♡ *"You are a naughty boy."* This statement is useless. It does not give the child any information on what they did wrong and only undermines their self-esteem. What you could say instead: *"You threw toys to your little brother. We do not accept this behavior in our home."*

♡ *"You are always so messy! You like dirt, don't you?"* This leaves the child wondering what the requested action is. A much better option could be*:* *"I bet you could sort your clothes and put your toys away by dinner!"*

♡ *"I am ashamed of you."* This sentence may cause a wound so deep, it may stay open forever. Whatever the cause, please, for the sake of your child, change the way you talk. You could say: *"When acting like this, you hurt me."*

If a child has done something that shouldn't have been done, has misbehaved, or has had to suffer the results of a wrong choice, it's necessary once again to avoid negative language patterns that attribute the failure to the child.

♡ *"It's all your fault!"* Instead, you could say, *"I know you didn't mean for that to happen. What went wrong?"* This phrasing sends the message that you have a positive idea of the kid regardless of the negative situation. You are saying that you know the kid didn't want to end up with the wrong results and demonstrate empathy and understanding.

## NEGATIVE COMMENTS

Many parents do an excellent job building up their kid's self-esteem while spending time with them. Then later, they ruin their outstanding work and let them overhear some negative comments. Obviously, as parents, we need to communicate with each other about our children and sometimes vent our frustrations. This is very common and normal. Just make sure that, when you do so, your kid is not able to overhear. No kid is young enough or busy enough to stop listening, especially when they hear their name.

## NOT PAYING ATTENTION

Not paying attention is something that unfortunately happens in every family now and then. We are so busy that sometimes we just cannot concentrate on other than ourselves.

In these moments, I find planning some quality time later in the day is useful for my children and me. I give them my full attention, enjoying their company, and I also have the opportunity to listen and get things that may worry my kids and do something about it immediately.

They may be statements doubting about their ability to do something, and I can express that I am sure they can perform the task successfully, or about their feelings, and I can acknowledge them and help them go past them.

Sometimes, no words and some cuddles will be more than enough. This kind of communication is one of the best to bond with our children, especially at a very young age.

# IDEAS TO COMMUNICATE BETTER

I believe that if we could observe ourselves from the outside, we would see that applying Montessori's principles is often easier than we think. We just lose ourselves our focus in the sea of everyday things.

So let's re-focus on some details that may improve communication in your family even more as it did in mine.

## ACCEPT KIDS AS THEY ARE

Children, especially when we grant them the freedom to do by themselves and the opportunity to explore the world as per Maria Montessori's teachings, will not always do things we like. Actually, more often than not, we will have to get used to something we weren't allowed to do as kids, and this will probably cause us strange feelings.

You may find yourself torn between a sense of feeling right (I am doing the best for my kid, this is the ultimate way to let them improve and grow as independent adults) and wrong (Look at that food on the ground! It's wrong to play with food, and things like that).

Just learn to accept your children as they are: beautiful human beings finding their place into the world.

And remember, from a very practical point of view, that you always have a chance to discuss an alternative with your kid and do not necessarily tolerate everything, especially behaviors or activities you don't like.

You could say, *"Honey, I don't like you doing 'this,' what about doing 'that'?"*

## GIVE THE RIGHT FEEDBACK

To better learn and improve, our children need our feedback. The best way to provide it is by making it descriptive because it will be easier to get even at a young age.

Describe what you see in a kid's picture, or describe what you like about it. For older kids, reiterate what you think they are saying to make sure you are both on the same wavelength.

You may also describe how it could be done better next time or just offer another way of tackling the problem, avoiding criticism at all. The next time the kid will have the opportunity to test your suggestion.

They may do it or not; in any case, appropriate feedback helps them gain self-confidence to try things by themselves.

## RARELY USE NO

This is one of the skills I developed almost immediately, as I actually find it pretty easy and quite stimulating.

"Rarely use NO" means "learn to say YES as much as possible," but... YES, to what exactly?

Every time we need to do something and tell it to our child, the standard reply is, *"I don't want to 'do that,' can I 'do this' instead?"* And my answer, standard as well, is *"YES! You can do that for 5 minutes; then we need to do this."*

It's a handy trick that allows you to let the child think they won the conflict when, in reality, you accepted a convenient trade-off.

I keep the NO for extreme cases where I cannot negotiate. My children know that when mom says no, it's because there's no viable alternative, and they accept without questioning (well, sometimes they do, but then accept).

The most important thing, and a useful suggestion from Maria Montessori, is to try avoiding interruptions. As I already explained in previous chapters, children tend to dislike changes, especially if they happen when an activity entirely absorbs their focus. So, unless there is a specific reason (typically: we are late, no matter how much planning I do, there are days that just seem flying like a rocket!), I tend to let them finish what they are doing so that they are then ready to listen to what I have to say.

You could say: *"Yes, you can keep playing with building blocks for 5 more minutes, then you'll put them back and go to bed"*.

Until a certain age, kids do not have a precise idea of what time is. My children never discussed that I let them stay for 15 minutes or 2 instead of 5; that has always been a plus.

## THE POWER OF LAUGH

Sometimes things get dark, no matter what effort you put in keeping things up, it just happens. You know those moments where everyone is sad, or angry, sometimes for reasons that are not clear. Maybe a bit less sleep, some words not appropriately positive, and the mood changes.

You need a total shift, and my suggestions is to laugh! I know it seems crazy, but a good laugh can reunite the whole family at the speed of light, lifting souls and relax everyone. With children, it works every time as every good distraction would do, so I suggest keeping this weapon under your belt and using it as soon as things don't go as you would like.

## MOTIVATE THROUGH CHALLENGES

If there's a thing children can't resist, it's competing in a challenge. They like to show their abilities and demonstrate how great they are at something. Hence, a challenge is an excellent way to encourage some behavior or activities without letting your kid feeling controlled or pushed.

For example, suppose you have a three-year-old daughter, and every time you need to leave by car, she doesn't want to sit at her place and fasten the belt. This is a perfect occasion for a challenge.

You could say, *"I bet that I can go faster than you! I bet I can lock the front door and come back to the car before you get into the backseat and buckle your seatbelt."*

Challenge is even more effective when you have more than one child. My daughters challenge themselves almost every night when preparing for bedtime. Who will be the first to put the pajamas on and climb onto the bed?

Next time you are experiencing some resistance, think:

*"What could I say to challenge them and let them do 'this'?"* Then try and look at what happens.

## CHANGE YOUR QUESTION

There is a question that is very common among some parents, and it is *"Why"*? Why did you break the vase?

Why did you pour the milk on the floor? Why? Why? Why?

Kids brain is developing and if there's a thing it can rarely do is answer this question. And the situation gets even worse if a parent starts asking the same thing repeatedly, maybe with a voice higher than usual.

In that case, the brain goes in protection mode, and the kid stops listening. I'm not telling this to say that we should tolerate every behavior; in fact, I'm here to telling you what works and what doesn't. In this case, I suggest changing the question. What happened is done, and we may never know why. It's essential that the child is aware of what they did, accepts responsibility, and does their best to mend the damage.

A more effective approach is asking, *"What are we going to do about it?"* Then listen to what your kid says. Even at a young age, they try to reason and figure out a way to solve the problem and act on it.

# EFFECTIVE COMMUNICATION

As parents, we need to remind ourselves that our kids learn from what we say and how we say it even if their **cognitive skills** are not fully developed.

## ♡ EXCLUSIVE LISTENING

Dedicate your **complete attention** to them and total focus on the conversation every time you can. By making exclusive listening a priority, your kid will feel **important and heard**.

## ♡ MUTUAL RESPECT

By respecting our kid's needs and feelings, we will teach them, by example, how to respect us.

By appreciating and trying to understand things from **their perspective**, you will get a better understanding of why they have behaved in specific ways. We can find solutions to problems.

Let them **express every emotion**. Accept them, as long as the child does not hurt himself, others or starts damaging things. In this case, gently stop him saying something that acknowledges his discomfort but also puts a limit to it.

## ♡ EYE CONTACT

Eye contact is **crucial** for kids, especially at a young age, so physically get down to their level every time you need to communicate with them, especially if it's a moment of exclusive communication with no interruption.

## ♡ REPEAT WHAT YOU UNDERSTAND

This will encourage them to communicate even more and consolidating their talking and reasoning skills.

You can help your children by repeating in your own words **what you think they're saying and how they're feeling about it**. You may say: " *You mean that...?*" or "*You seem sad now. Does it mean that you don't want to ...?*"

## ♡ KEEP IT SIMPLE

Children have many limitations on the way they can process what you say to them. Young kids simply do not understand things they cannot see, hear, or touch while older ones are still developing the ability to think in more abstract ways.

**Communicate with kids in a basic way**: keep it simple and to the point. Use examples that they can relate to.

## ♡ DON'T PRAISE

Maria Montessori discouraged praise; in her vision, the child acts to develop their path, not to make us happy, not to get our approval. **Praise by itself is useless. Punishment is useless, as well.** A child shouldn't be forced to do something just because they fear our reaction.

## ♡ MANAGE CONFLICTS

When a conflict arises, ask yourself:

♡ Is my child's idea somehow acceptable, even if very far from mine?

♡ Is it something worth spending time to mediate, teaching them how to find a solution by themselves?

**Stimulate the kid to find a solution by themselves.** We could say, *"I understand your position, but unfortunately, this is not possible. What do you think we can do to solve this?"*

## ♡ COMMUNICATION MISTAKES

Some mistakes may cause children to feel bad about themselves and not properly aiding their healthy growth.

♡ **Wrong language patterns** Most damaging language patterns include words like: always, never, every time, all, etc. They state something which seems universally and unconditionally true, and this is a big problem.

**Describe the problematic situation as it is here and now.**

*"You are mean and never show me respect"* You could say instead: *"You hurt my feelings, I don't want to treat me like that."*

Another wrong pattern is **talking about the identity of the child** in general rather the behavior, action or words, etc. that are currently problematic like:

*"You are a naughty boy."* This statement does not give the child any information on what he did wrong and undermines their self-esteem. You could say instead: *"You threw toys to your little brother. We do not accept this behavior in our home."*

♡ **Negative comments**. Be sure to talk when your child is not able to overhear. No kid is young enough or busy enough to stop listening, especially when they hear their name.

♡ **Not paying attention:** Plan some quality time every day to give them full attention, enjoying your children's company. Listen and get things that may worry your kids and do something about it immediately.

## ♡ IDEAS TO COMMUNICATE BETTER

Let's focus on some details that may improve communication in your family even more.

### ♡ Accept kids as they are

Children will not always do things we like.

Just learn to accept them as they are. Remember that you always have a chance to discuss an **alternative** with your kid and do not necessarily tolerate everything, especially behaviors or activities you don't like.

### ♡ Give the right feedback

To better learn and improve, our children need our feedback. **Making it descriptive**, it will be easier to get even at a young age. E.g., Describe what you see in a kid's picture, or describe what you like about it.

### ♡ Rarely use NO

Learn how to communicate so that your kids have **the impression you say NO very rarely.** This means to learn a basic trick to let them think they got what they want.

*"Yes, you can keep playing with building blocks for 5 more minutes, then you'll put them back and go to bed".*

♡ **The power of laugh:** a good laugh can reunite the whole family at the speed of light, lifting souls and relax everyone. With children, **it works every time** as every good distraction would do; use it as soon as things don't go as you would like.

♡ **Motivate through challenge** Children like to **show their abilities** and demonstrate how great they are at things. Hence, a challenge is an excellent way to encourage some behaviors or activities without letting your kid feeling controlled or pushed.

♡ **Change your question** Don't ask, "why?". Kids brain is developing and if there's a thing they can't do is answer this question. And the situation gets even worse if a parent starts asking the same thing repeatedly, maybe with a voice higher than usual. A more effective approach would be to **accept that the issue happened and ask how to move past it:** *"What are we going to do about it?".*

# CHAPTER 8

# ACTIVITIES FOR KIDS

Play is the work of the child.

— Maria Montessori

A major way kids collect and process new information is through play in a suitable environment. We already examined how to adapt your home to create a perfect learning and playing arena.

Now, let's look at some Montessori activities to reinforce old skills and encourage new ones. The reason why they are so effective is that they are both fun and educational. Children enjoying what they're doing have an open mind, and being receptive and relaxed is the perfect condition for learning.

Active participation in everyday life activities allows the kid to think logically, sequencing the steps needed to perform a given task. Each task completed builds self-esteem. When the kid's mind and body are active, his intellect can develop fully.

Natural supplies, imaginative actions, and allowing your kid to explore the world independently are all it takes to bring the Montessori approach in your house and delve into new experiences. As a parent, your role is to observe and gently guide, but parents are more than welcome to join in.

## WHAT ARE MONTESSORI ACTIVITIES?

Montessori activities are studied to support children through their different development stages (or "sensitive periods," as seen in the related chapter) and present several characteristics:

- ♡ They encourage a single ability at a time
- ♡ They use mainly natural materials (like wood or paper) and commonly used household items
- ♡ They include several phases, and a child can complete the activity from the beginning to the end or, depending on their skills, stop at an intermediate step until completely mastered
- ♡ They typically include a phase to put back the activity at its place to enforce children's love for order. The activity is usually put in a basket or a tray for easy access. If you have little space, you may want to use easy to open, stackable boxes and identify each activity with an image on the front.
- ♡ Cleaning materials are often included: clothes, sponges, brush, and dustpan.
- ♡ They are supposed to be shown from an adult, slowly, in silence, and several times until the child can work alone.

# ACTIVITIES

"The best instruction is that which uses the least words
sufficient for the task."

— Maria Montessori

Montessori activities have been categorized so that you can develop different skills every time.

I also included some activities that develop the same skills as the Montessori ones from a different perspective, with a little more adult presence, which is essential at a very young age when still learning all the basics.

The goal is obviously to support children's development and independence.

## IMPORTANT TIPS

♡ As we learned in the previous chapters, children learn by repetition. It's essential to allow enough time and let them repeatedly try until they master each activity successfully. Do not interrupt and remember that the action is more important than its perfection. Improvement will come in time through trial and error.

♡ Creativity is essential, so if a child uses materials in a way that is not the one they "should," just let them experiment ad long as they don't cause any damage to materials and other people.

♡ It's better to select a few activities after observing the child's level of development and cues. Remember that in a Montessori environment, activities are displayed in order of difficulty. Parents can change them as long as they become too easy to keep their interest up.

♡ It's ok to leave the child experience boredom from time to time because it's a moment where creativity has a boost, and new cerebral connections are made. Your child will push themselves to get out of this status, exploring new things.

♡ <u>**ALWAYS**</u> ♡

<u>**KEEP YOUR CHILD UNDER SUPERVISION**</u>

Some activities may include small parts.

# FINE AND GROSS MOTOR SKILLS

## FINE MOTOR SKILLS

♡ Manipulate building blocks. There are endless possibilities suitable for every age: sort them by colors, shapes, dimensions. Create rows, simple and complex structures, houses, skyscrapers, castles, etc.

♡ Puzzles, from the ones with bigger pieces and knobs, to smaller and more complex ones. The child will be ready to move to the next level when they complete the puzzle with no effort.

♡ Cut and paste with scissors and paper. Give old newspapers/magazines/supermarket flyers to cut strips, confetti, or shapes. Learn to cut similar things (e.g., faces, foods, etc.). Glue them together or on a sheet of paper to create a composition.

♡ Use playdough (preferably homemade, see page 197) and kinetic sand. Manipulate with hands or tools like a rolling pin and cookie cutters of different shapes.

♡ Open and close zippers, snap buttons, standard buttons. Use old clothes, adequately cut, or sew all the items on the same piece of fabric so that the child can experiment with different kinds of movements.

♡ Open and close locks, using a latch board (you can buy it or do it with some inexpensive materials from any DIY store)

♡ Recognize different objects in a bag, just with a touch. Depending on age, use simple or complex shapes. Use kitchen tools or other safe items you already have at home.

♡ Stack cups (plastic or steel ones).

♡ Empty a toy/clothes basket (and fill it back again).

♡ Arrange a basket or a box with several objects to observe with a magnifying glass. Natural items like shells, leaves, rocks of different shapes, and sizes capture curiosity instantly.

♡ Use a mortar and pestle to grind seeds/raisins or other food.

♡ Stack rings on a stacking toy. Growing older, the child will be able to order the rings by their dimension.

♡ Open and close various containers. The child may start from containers that already have their matching lid, and when they're older, they learn to match containers and lid from the ones in a basket.

♡ Moving dry materials (oats, rice, semolina flour, or other edible/non-edible options) from one container to another. The child will inevitably drop some on the table and floor, show them how to clean with the proper tools. This kind of activity is crucial for hand-eye coordination and for learning how to keep the workspace tidy. Cleaning will be a normalized step of it, in their charge.

♡ Move water from one container to another. Choose different types of containers with large and small openings to increase difficulty. Always include clothes or a sponge and teach how to dry the water that will inevitably drop.

♡ Use a shape sorting toy. Include blocks of different shapes (cylinder, cube, etc.) and let them choose the right hole to insert them.

♡ Drop coins into a piggy bank; alternatively, use popsicle sticks, cards, or other flat items and a box where you cut a slit. The smaller the slit, the hardest the activity. Let the child select what to drop among things with different thicknesses.

♡ Kneading dough and cooking bread or cookies is an excellent exercise for their hand muscles.

## GROSS MOTOR SKILLS

♡ Walk, run, jump.

♡ Ride a bike or a scooter, slide, swing, hang from a tree.

♡ Play with a ball using feet or hands, hit it with a racket, or throw it in a basket. (Use balls of different dimensions).

♡ Carry their chair or table from one point of the room to another.

# LANGUAGE

♡ Read books, from the ones including just pictures, to single words, to phrases/rhymes. Teach how to select a book, how to turn pages, how to put it back.

♡ Sing songs with your child.

♡ Create treasure baskets with items to explore a single letter of the alphabet (e.g., some ideas for items starting with G:  a pair of glasses, a giraffe, a goat, a gorilla, a grasshopper, a goldfish,  a green item and a gold one, a picture of a ghost, a card showing a letter "G", etc. )

♡ Go for a walk (inside your home or outside) and repeat the words of the things you see. Remember to speak slowly and let the child repeat. The next step is to ask the child to identify objects by pronouncing the word.

♡ Use cards with pictures to expand vocabulary. Use figures to represent the word (e.g., animals, shapes, etc.). Ask for the word related to the card.

# ART AND CREATIVITY

♡ Doodle/Color using wax crayons and pencils.

♡ Paint with finger paint, watercolors, tempera colors. Learn how to mix colors and use an easel.

♡ Paint 3D surfaces, like Styrofoam balls or figures, carton boxes, etc.

♡ Paint bubble wrap then put a clean sheet of paper on to stamp the color onto it. Let dry and use for other creative activities.

♡ Select simple natural materials in your yard and use them for beautiful projects. They can be glued together or onto something. Put flat items like leaves or feathers under a sheet of paper, and using a wax crayon, create a lovely imprint.

♡ Use clay. Form shapes using hands and tools like cookie cutters. Let them dry them, then paint them. Propose to develop a theme, creating different shapes (e. Christmas, Halloween, etc.) and let them follow their fantasy. Offer additional items for decoration: glitters, stickers, etc.

♡ Engage kids in imaginative play. Put all your children's costumes in a trunk and let them choose who they want to be today. They will practice dress up, boost creative thinking, and social interaction.

## MUSIC AND MATH

♡ Fill small containers with screw cap with rice/beans/etc. and play them like maracas. Let the child fill the containers and experiment with the different sounds given by different quantities of grains in them.

♡ Play whistle, trumpet, mouth organ, tambourine.

♡ Play drum or xylophone. If you don't have any, turn a pot upside down and let the child hit it with a wooden spoon or other suitable items to make a sound.

♡ Let the child order some glasses on the table, pour a different quantity of water in each one, and test with a butter knife the gentle sound each glass makes.

♡ Order items from the smallest to the biggest or vice versa. The next step may be, sort the items by color and then order them by dimension.

♡ Fill a lunch box. Show how to dispose of food with order and estimate the number of items that will fit into the box's space and depth. Later they may even count the number of grapes in their container while they eat them.

♡ Learn math by counting pebbles or stacking rocks.

♡ At the supermarket, look at price labels and identify numbers. Count items in the cart.

♡ Cook together. Let the child weight ingredients and confront the number on the scale with the number on the recipe. Choose a recipe for two people and ask what to do with ingredients to cook for four people.

♡ Counting numbers on a journey. Suggest an item (trees, red cars, blue things that move, etc.) or let them choose by themselves and count them during the journey. If there is more than a child, set up a challenge.

♡ Counting and sorting items with the same colors. You could use pebbles, let the child color it, and then use it as an activity. You may also use some containers to identify with different colors to put the related pebbles.

## PRACTICAL LIFE

♡ Brush teeth, wash hands, brush hair, dress up.

♡ Learn to tie shoes

♡ Put dirty clothes in the laundry basket, sort them by color, and put them into the washing machine.

♡ Sort clean laundry: napkins, underwear, pair socks.

♡ Carry plates, glasses, cutlery, napkins to the table. Set up the table. Clear it.

♡ Wash/clean plates, cutlery, tables, floor, windows. Make space for their tools or set up a cleaning caddy with a wash fabric, wipes, brush, dustpan, and water sprayer.

♡ Fill the cat's (or other animal's) bowl.

♡ Plant seeds in the garden or a vase using proper gardening tools. Water plants/flowers, fill the watering can. Put it back.

♡ Cut flowers and arrange them in a container with water.

♡ Select products from a visual shopping list, pick them up (in the right amount), and add them to the supermarket cart.

♡ Explore the little treasure of nature: bright-green grass, ribbed leaves, perfumed blossoms. Let the child absorb the quietness and the beauty of nature.

# USEFUL MATERIALS

In case you don't have much space to place materials, you may evaluate a busy board, which includes several activities for toddlers. As the child grows up, you may want to keep it simple and stack a few light boxes with a picture showing the activity inside to select by themselves.

Please note that everyday materials you already have at home are enough to arrange many exciting activities. Children love to experiment with the items they see in our hands every day. They are unique because mom and dad use them!

When on a budget (and also when loving DIY!), remember that it's possible to buy unfinished wood supplies online (beads, peg people, animals, shapes, wooden eggs, blocks, etc.) and paint them with non-toxic paint. There are several cheap brands around, so you will be able to create your own sets at a sustainable price.

As far as activities to buy, there are so many attractive options out there that making a complete list may take several pages, and it's out of the purpose of this book. I selected some of the choices I would make today.

Always remember that if your children already attend a Montessori school, it's essential to differentiate the materials between the ones at home and the ones at school.

♡ Toys with knobs, handles, buttons

♡ Simple animal, people, or vehicle puzzles with large pieces

♡ Children's picture books that are colorful and eye-catching

♡ Picture cards

♡ Toys with music, different sounds, and songs

♡ Push/pull objects that encourage children to move around

♡ Toys that educate them with a sense of big and small, tall and short, heavy and light.

♡ Concepts in math and science including counting, relating the number to the quantity and vice versa, simple measurements and balance

♡ Toys that encourage dramatic/imaginary play

♡ Storybooks that encourage the kid to participate - these are books that have simple words, short phrases, and bigger fonts

♡ Balls, skipping ropes, hula hoops

♡ Ride-on toys and bicycles for older toddlers.

One last note.

Several non-Montessori toys are very useful and can be easily alternated to Montessori ones to keep the child's interest high—for example, animal figurines Lego, toy cars, trains, board games.

## EDIBLE 5-MINUTE PLAYDOUGH RECIPE

Commercial playdough is full of nasty ingredients. Considering this and its price, I honestly prefer to prepare it at home in 5 minutes. It's easy, it's edible, and it's cheap. I stopped worrying about my daughters mixing colors a long time ago because I can prepare a new batch a soon as I need it.

Here the ingredients, enough for 2 children to play:

# 5-MINUTE PLAYDOUGH RECIPE

♡ **Water:** 2 cups

♡ **Vegetable oil:** 2 tbsp.

♡ **Flour:** 2 cups

♡ **Salt:** 1/2 cup

♡ **Cream of tartar:** 4 tbsp.

♡ **Food colorings:** Choose the ones your children love the most or keep the dough natural and don't add any.

Mix dry ingredients in a pot, add water and vegetable oil slowly and mix well to avoid lumps.

Divide the quantity into two parts and combine two different food coloring (optional).

Turn on the heat and cook for 3 minutes until the dough reaches the desired consistency, let it cool.

Knead the dough a bit, then form a ball and store it in a container.

# A LETTER TO PARENTS

Self-care is giving the world the best of you, instead of what's left of you.

— Katie Reed

We cannot control what happens outside, but we can control how we react to it. In this book, we put the child first, but it's important to remember that parents' wellbeing is fundamental too. Having our private relax time, maybe when kids are sleeping, is essential as when we are too stressed we are victims of anxiety, fatigue, and problems. Without charging our batteries effectively on a daily basis, it becomes challenging, if not impossible, to manage day-by-day situations, especially if kids are very young.

Focusing on our goals and desires, using the techniques we like the most, from yoga to meditation, from sport to journaling, is beneficial to all the family and is an essential example for our children.

Remember to slow down sometimes; changing pace is often beneficial for everyone.

Remember that, like our children, we may make mistakes and that, just like them, we always have the possibility to apologize and re-start from a new page.

A big hug to all of you. I wish you a pleasant journey through parenting, made of discoveries, fun, laugh, and love!

Enjoy!

Maggie♥

# REFERENCE

Montessori, M. (1948). The Discovery of the Child

Montessori, M. (1949). The Absorbent Mind

Montessori, M. (1914). Dr. Montessori's Own Handbook

Ajzen, I. (1988). Attitudes, personality, and behavior. Chicago: The Dorsey Press.

Burnett, P. (1999). The impact of teachers' praise on students' self-talk and self-concepts. New South Wales, Aus: Teaching and Teacher Education. Retrieved September 15, 2005, from ERIC database.

Canadian Education Act. (1997) Retrieved Sep. 14, 2005, from http://www.gnb.ca/acts/acts/e-01-12.htm

Di Giulio, R. (2001). Educate, medicate, or litigate? What teachers, parents, and administrators must do about student behavior. California, US: Educational Management. Retrieved September 15, 2005, from ERIC database.

Doctor, S. (1997). Creating a positive school climate. Towards Inclusion: Tapping Hidden Strengths, 3. http://www.edu.gov.mb.ca/ks4/specedu/fas/pdf/3.pdf

Faber, A. and Maizlish, E (1980). How to talk so kids will listen and listen so kids will talk.

Glatt, F. J. (2003). Retrieved Sep. 14, 2005, from Reading, is FUNdamental from http://www.sandralreading.com.

Johnson, C., Templeton, R., and Guofang, W. (2000). Pathways to peace: promoting non-violent learning environments. Chicago: Elementary and Early Childhood Education. Retrieved September 16, 2005, from ERIC database.

Muijs, D., Harris A., Chapman C., and Stoll, L. (2004). Improving schools in socioeconomically disadvantaged areas--a review of research evidence. School Effectiveness and School Improvement, 15(2), 149-175.

Made in the USA
Coppell, TX
16 October 2021